orphan B·L·O·C·K quilts

KRAUSE PUBLICATIONS
CINCINNATI, OHIO

orphan B·L·O·C·K quilts

making a home *for* antique, vintage, collectible *&* leftover quilt blocks

TRICIA LYNN MALONEY

kp

KRAUSE PUBLICATIONS
CINCINNATI, OHIO

Orphan Block Quilts. Copyright © 2010 by Tricia Lynn Maloney. Manufactured in China. All rights reserved. No part of this book may be reproduced in any form or by any electronic or mechanical means including information storage and retrieval systems without permission in writing from the publisher, except by a reviewer who may quote brief passages in a review. Published by Krause Publications, a division of F+W Media, Inc., 4700 East Galbraith Road, Cincinnati, Ohio, 45236. (800) 289-0963. First Edition.

www.fwmedia.com

14 13 12 11 10   5 4 3 2 1

Distributed in Canada by Fraser Direct
100 Armstrong Avenue
Georgetown, ON, Canada L7G 5S4
Tel: (905) 877-4411

Distributed in the U.K. and Europe by David & Charles
Brunel House, Newton Abbot, Devon, TQ12 4PU, England
Tel: (+44) 1626 323200, Fax: (+44) 1626 323319
Email: postmaster@davidandcharles.co.uk

Distributed in Australia by Capricorn Link
P.O. Box 704, S. Windsor NSW, 2756 Australia
Tel: (02) 4577-3555

Library of Congress Cataloging in Publication Data
Maloney, Tricia Lynn
 Orphan block quilts : making a home for antique, vintage, collectible, and leftover quilt blocks / Tricia Lynn Maloney.
   p. cm.
 Includes index.
 ISBN-13: 978-1-4402-0552-1 (pbk. : alk. paper)
 ISBN-10: 1-4402-0552-3 (pbk. : alk. paper)
 1. Patchwork. 2. Quilting. I. Title.

 TT835.M272132 2010
 746.46--dc22
                                           2010013848

Edited by Vanessa Lyman, Amy Jeynes
Designed by Michelle Thompson, Hotiron Creative
Production coordinated by Greg Nock
Photography by Ric Deliantoni, unless otherwise noted

❖ metric *conversion* chart

To convert	to	multiply by
Inches	Centimeters	2.54
Centimeters	Inches	0.4
Feet	Centimeters	30.5
Centimeters	Feet	0.03
Yards	Meters	0.9
Meters	Yards	1.1

❖ about *the* author

Tricia Lynn Maloney began working with antique textiles in a local museum while pursuing a degree at Allegheny College. Later she went into the field of education and holds a Masters in elementary education/childhood education. Tricia has worked in a quilt shop and designs her own patterns and quilts, selling locally and online. She teaches quilt classes in hand-dyeing fabrics, purse making, designing quilts and free motion quilting. Additionally, she has co-taught an annual 12-month quilt program since 2007. Tricia is an officer of her quilt guild, Country Charms.

✤ dedication

Photo of Louetta Shoemaker Hoffman
courtesy of Nancy S. Nyilyk

This book is dedicated to:

Quilters of the past like Louetta
Shoemaker Hoffman, Ausie Shutt, and
my great grandmothers, Mary Dain
Maloney and Emma Ferlin Picard

Quilters of today like my dear friends
Cathey Laird, Leslie Lattner, Mary Lee
Minnis and my fellow guild members

And the Quilters of tomorrow,
perhaps my nieces Meghan and
Morgan Cronin

Also, Mom and Dad. Thanks.

✤ acknowledgements

My editor, Vanessa Lyman, for her vision, energy, and creativity. Also, thank you to all of the wonderful people at Krause who helped make this book a reality. Cathey Laird, Leslie Lattner and Mary Lee Minnis for being the best friends in the whole world —always there to offer suggestions, bind quilts, piece tops and just listen. Designer and fellow author, Cheryl Weiderspahn, for showing me the way, answering hundreds of questions, providing guidance and support, and most of all for her friendship. My fellow quilt guild members for their support and for gifting me with orphan quilt blocks. Barb Shuck and Cindy Beggs for not only their beautiful machine quilting but also for giving me stacks of orphan blocks. Gaynel Sickles for her exquisite machine quilting. The 2009 Victory Class Ladies for bearing with me during the writing and creating process and offering great suggestions along the way. Gail Baker, my local quilt shop owner and friend, for her encouragement and support. Nancy Nyilyk for helping me to get to know her grandmother, Louetta Shoemaker Hoffman. Barbara Beckwith and Joanne Weiss for sharing their grandmother, Ausie Shutt. Becky Van Kleeck for ushering me into the world of quilts. Peg Weymer for sharing her knowledge of antique quilts and fabrics during my museum days. Dr. Paula Treckel for nurturing my love of history and Mrs. Beth Wilcox for inspiring me to write. And finally to my family—for listening, critiquing and filling in when deadlines approached.

table *of* contents

working *with* orphan blocks

· 1 ·

An orphan block is simply any quilt block that hasn't found a home in a completed quilt yet. Orphan blocks can be old, new, in good condition or poor; they can be well pieced or badly pieced; attractive or unappealing; pieced or appliquéd. They can be signed by the maker or made by unknown hands. They can even be from last month's UFO (Unfinished Fabric Object). They can be yours or someone else's.

This book shows you how to take those lost, unused or perhaps even unloved blocks and make a home for them. Any abandoned block can become part of a one-of-a-kind, beloved quilt. You don't necessarily need to have lots of blocks—some projects start with just one. It's simply a matter of knowing how to create the right setting. The projects in this book teach you to do that.

Making an orphan block quilt is an amazing experience! It's fun, exciting, challenging and creative. When you begin the process, you never know exactly where you will end up. You may think you know what the final project will look like, but often the project takes you on a few unexpected side roads along the way. Part of the enjoyment is the anticipation of not quite knowing what the final result will be. If you are fortunate enough to have signature blocks signed by the maker(s), you might even discover a lost quilter with a little basic research. This, of course, could lead your project in an entirely new direction.

A completed orphan block quilt can be:

- A tangible reminder of times enjoyed with the beloved friend or family member who made the blocks.

- A connection to ancestors you never knew.

- A way to hear the voices of quilters whose names are long forgotten but whose personalities live on in their handiwork.

And it's always great fun to hunt for vintage, reproduction, or new fabrics to complement an old piece or evoke the style of the era when the orphan blocks were made.

Whether your orphan quilt blocks are modern or antique, this section will show you how to select suitable blocks and get them ready for your own orphan block quilt project.

Let's get started!

Old Maid's Puzzle circa 1935

Nine Patch circa 1920

Eight Point Star circa 1995

finding orphan
quilt blocks

Before making quilts, you need to find the blocks! Where can you find orphans?

Your Stash

The first place to look for orphan blocks is in your own stash. Probably, you'll only find modern orphans, but who knows, perhaps you'll find a few antique orphans lurking about. If you're like me, you have lots of unfinished fabric objects (UFO's) and these might yield orphans. So, look for extra blocks, sampler quilts that were never finished, blocks that were ugly and never found their way into a project, sample blocks from projects you never made, or even projects in which you didn't make enough blocks and thus never completed the quilt.

Flea Markets

Flea markets are like garage sales and auctions combined. If you attend a flea market, you can look at what each vendor has to sell. Some items will have prices, others will be unmarked. If the item is unmarked, you might ask the vendor, "What's your best price?" Now, the fun part about flea markets is that prices are rarely fixed. If you're interested and the price seems fair to you, pay it; however, if it seems high, make a counteroffer. I have learned that it is often very persuasive to have the exact amount of your offer (cash of course) in your hand when you make it. (Please note that this technique can also help you at garage sales.) Keep in mind that the vendor may counter your offer with one of his own. Another important thing to remember about flea markets is that if you want it, buy it when you see it. If you go back later to try to get a better deal, chances are it has already been sold to someone else.

Antique Dealers, Shops and Shows

If you're looking for antique orphans, antique dealers are a wonderful resource. Most of the time, dealers have their own specialties and may even devalue items that are not part of that specialty. Call around, stop and visit shops in your area and on your travels—you'll be surprised about the unfinished quilt blocks and even quilt tops that you find. Often, prices will be reasonable—even cheap. Making friends with a dealer is a great idea. As he goes to sales and shows, he will most likely keep you in mind when spotting quilt items which may interest you, the customer. Checking out antique shows will help you to get to know antique dealers both in and out of your area.

Quilt Shops and Shows

Quilt shop owners often know of or have antique blocks for sale. People who inherit Grandma's stash often seek the advice of local quilt shop owners. If the shop owner is a friend of yours, chances are she will connect the quilt stash owner to you or she will call you first to tell you about the awesome new antique blocks she has on consignment. Shop owners might even come into modern block collections.

Professional long-arm machine and hand quilters are often in the same position. If you make quilts and have them quilted by a professional long arm quilter or hand quilter or know one in your local area, talk to her (or him) about what you're looking for. Sometimes, they're the recipients of family stashes of quilt treasures, including blocks and fabrics. Or, they might be able to tell customers about your mission and what you're looking for.

As for quilt shows, not only do you get to see amazing works of art, you might be surprised at what the vendors are offering for sale.

Friends and Family

Talk to everyone around you, let them know what you are looking for, and what you would be willing to spend on specific items. Fifty people looking for quilt blocks are more likely to find them than just one person. This works well for both modern and antique blocks because quilting friends and family have stashes, too! Besides, nonquilting family or friends might have inherited Grandma's quilt stash and were looking for someone to treasure it because they don't want it, but can't just toss it out, either. Who knows, you might even inherit some distant relative's quilt stash.

Quilt Guilds

Guilds are like your quilt family. Join one if you haven't already. Tell them what you're looking for. If they have it, most likely they will share it with you.

Garage and Yard Sales

These can be great places to find both modern and antique quilt items, but I caution you to remember that this resource can be very hit or miss. Check out your local newspaper's garage sale ads. Look for listings that include fabric, material, quilting, sewing, etc., but beware that ads can be misleading or the items might already be gone by the time you get there. But have heart, some of my best finds have been at local garage sales.

Auctions

Auctions are very much like garage sales. It's a good idea to look at the auction ads in your local paper before checking an auction out. If you see any mention of quilts, visit the auction before it starts so that you can look around and get a feel for what is offered for sale and what you are willing to spend, if you are interested.

Always have a set limit in mind for each item that you are interested in and write it down! Do not get sucked into the frenzy of bidding and go beyond your means.

If the auction ad does not list quilts, there are some things to look for that could indicate the presence of quilt items. Look for the mention of sewing machines, linens, fabric, and the like. If these things are mentioned, there may be boxes of unfinished quilt blocks or tops just waiting for you.

Check out the auction thoroughly before it begins and make sure you examine the contents of every box in the box lot section.

Internet and Internet Auctions

The Internet is also a source, but I would approach this one carefully. It is easy to be tricked because you cannot see the exact condition of the items in a photograph and items can be misrepresented intentionally or quite by accident. Stick with reputable Internet dealers (ask for recommendations from local antique dealers, shop owners, friends, etc.) Make sure that, if you are buying something from a seller or dealer on the Internet, you understand all the costs and return policies, if there are any. If this is a source that you are interested in, my advice would be to try it, but don't spend much money until you gain some Internet savvy, just in case what you thought you bought wasn't what you received in the mail.

Internet auctions combine the convenience of the Internet with the excitement of an auction. If you are interested in bidding on items on auction sites, do your homework. Read the site policies and rules. Ask questions if you need to. Once you find an item that you're interested in bidding on, carefully review all of the photos and read all information provided by the seller including complete descriptions and condition, payment instructions, shipping and handling, and any other fees. If you are unsure, ask questions before you bid.

Remember, the search is often as much fun as the actual find. Happy hunting!

11

Six Point String Star circa 1950

Nine Patch Variation circa 1920

Grandmother's Flower circa 1930

identify suitable common blocks

Now you are searching for your own orphan quilt blocks. You're looking in your stash, sifting through boxes in grandma's attic, contacting local quilt and antique shops, checking out the Internet auctions, and stopping at every garage sale in your area. Suddenly, you have your very own collection of orphan quilt blocks.

So, what's next? What should you do when you find old blocks you might like to rework into an orphan block quilt?

Do nothing until you are sure the blocks aren't rare or otherwise valuable. This book is not about restoration and conservation of rare or special quilt blocks. Such work must be handled by professionals. Even with the best of intentions, the value of an historic or otherwise significant piece could be destroyed by cleaning, altering or changing the original piece.

Read on for a basic introduction to the differences between common and rare blocks. If you have any doubt as to the value of a quilt block, consult a conservator or other textile professional. Your local quilt guild, quilt or antique shop, or museum can help you locate one.

❖ terms *to* know

Antique block: a quilt block more than 99 years old

Collectible block: any quilt block that is collected; can be old or new

Common block: a quilt block intended for regular daily use

Finished size: the size of a piece after it is completed; quilt blocks generally have a ¼" seam allowance on all sides, so the finished size of a quilt block is the dimensions of the unfinished block minus the seam allowances (for example, a 9½" block would be finished at 9")

Leftover block: a surplus quilt block from a specific project

Modern block: a quilt block newer than 40 years old, often interchangeable with contemporary

Orphan block: a quilt block that is not part of a finished quilt project

Provenance: information consisting of location, maker, era, materials, design

Rare block: a quilt block that is uncommon due to its age, maker, design or historical significance

Setting: the frame around the quilt blocks

Set in: sewing a quilt piece into the corner, or angle, formed by two earlier- joined pieces

Signature block: a quilt block with a signature inked or stitched on it; also sometimes called an album or friendship block

UFO: Unfinished Fabric Object, or a project started but not completed

Vintage block: a quilt block from 40-99 years old

Common Blocks

The projects in this book are intended to be worked using ordinary, everyday blocks, also called "common blocks." A common block is:

• **Intended for regular daily use (i.e., for warmth or comfort).** Sometimes people call completed quilts made with this type of block "utility quilts." The blocks are often of simple designs and are generally made with cotton fabrics and thread. By contrast, a quilt created as a showpiece has some value as an art object and therefore should not be casually transformed into another piece. "Art quilt" orphan blocks may not be made of sturdy cotton fabrics and thread, but instead of delicate silks or other fabrics with the possibility of fragile embellishments.

• **Not rare in terms of provenance.** Provenance means its source of origin which would include such things as the maker(s), fabric(s), place it was made, era, even the design(s). For example, what if you found a set of signed quilt blocks with signatures of several historic women along with a block signed with the name of your great-grandmother, and you wanted to know if you could make an orphan quilt out of them. You would need to check the authenticity of the signatures and also consult a textile professional to determine what would be appropriate for this set of blocks.

• **Not valuable in terms of its age.** Generally speaking, the older a quilt block, the more likely it could be rare. For example, there are relatively few surviving quilts from before the early 1800s. This may be attributed to scarcity/expense of fabric, quilts being "used up" and then discarded, instability of early fabric dyes, and age. The majority of common blocks in my collection date from after the American Civil War, when fabric was inexpensive and women made quilts to be used. The blocks that I use in orphan quilts are frequently misshapen, soiled and poorly-pieced. This, of course, does not mean that all soiled blocks have no value—this would depend on other factors, particularly provenance. If you are unsure, check with a professional.

• **Not rare in terms of pattern.** Some patterns and designs are more desirable than others. For example, if you found a stack of 1850s hand appliquéd Baltimore Album blocks, they may be more valuable left as-is than if you completed them into a quilt. Common blocks are often made of simple designs such as nine patch, four patch, stars, strips, flying geese, log cabins, etc.

Remember, if there is any doubt as to whether a quilt block is suitable for the projects in this book, err on the side of caution and consult a professional.

❖ preparation *of* orphan blocks

1 Put on cotton gloves to keep the block clean.

2 Inspect both sides of the block for each of the following:

Piecing
• Seams should be tight and not frayed or separated. Check for tightness by tugging gently on the block with both hands. If the seams separate or thread loosens, you may need to re-sew seams.
• If hand-pieced, stitches should be small and uniform.
• Adequate seam allowances (¼" is the norm).

Fabrics
• Fabrics should be free of holes, tears, stains, musty or other odors, or bleeding colors.
• Fabrics should be good quality (not extremely thin or loosely woven).

Dimensions and Squareness
• Measure. The instructions in the project section refer to the finished size of orphan blocks; take into account the ¼" seam allowance on all sides.

• Check squareness. Lay the block on a flat surface, and gently smooth it out. Eyeball the block briefly. Does it look relatively square? Does it lay flat? Check its actual size using a gridded ruler larger than the block (if the block is large, you may need to carefully measure each side separately and compare the dimensions).

Any Other Problems
• Seek professional advice from a textile conservator. Your local quilt guild, quilt or antique shop, or museum can recommend one.

3 Clean all blocks before proceeding with a quilt project, even if they appear to be clean. (See page 16.) It's best to clean the blocks before repairing because the blocks might not survive the cleaning process. It's better to know that right away.

4 Make any needed repairs (see page 18) after cleaning.

Six Point String Star circa 1950

Grandmother's Flower Garden circa 1930

Hanging Basket circa 1930

inspecting your
blocks

Whether your orphan blocks are antique, vintage or modern, there are some common problems you'll identify. Follow the checklist on the previous page to examine your blocks. Antique blocks can have more complex problems than modern blocks. If you're not sure of your skills as a doctor for sick quilt blocks, seek professional advice before attempting repairs.

Examine Front and Back

Look carefully at both the front and back of the quilt block. This orphan, a Six Point String Star block (see block in upper left margin), reveals hand-stitched seams on the back. The stitches are regular, with an occasional backstitch for stability, even if the stitching is not tiny. It also shows fragments of paper caught in the seams, a clue that the fabrics were originally sewn to a paper foundation. The seam allowances appear to be adequate even if they aren't all exactly the same. The outer edges seem to be a bit ragged, but not so bad that the edges could not be turned under and appliquéd to a background fabric.

Poor-Quality Fabrics

The Basket block on the left uses a thin, gauzy, nearly transparent fabric that shows the underlying seams. The Nine Patch block on the right uses fabric with an extremely loose weave. The fabrics in these two blocks are not sturdy enough for use. Either replace the poor-quality fabric (see page 18) or do not use the block.

Separated Seams

Notice the split between patches in these two blocks, a Nine Patch on the left and a Sixteen Patch on the right. If the thread is broken, the seams can easily be resewn on the original seam lines. If the seams are separated due to fraying, see Frayed Seams, below. If the fabric itself is split, it can be replaced with a similar piece of fabric.

Frayed Seams

Fraying can occur from poor quality fabrics, rough handling or frequent washing. The Double Nine Patch block on the left even has a split seam due to fraying. The Monkey Wrench block (back shown) on the right has such badly-frayed edges that there is no outer ¼" seam allowance. It is possible that the Nine Patch might be repairable by reinforcing all of the seams. As for the Churn Dash block, the best solution would be to take the block apart, re-cut all of the pieces smaller, and then sew the block back together. The block would be smaller than the original dimensions, but it would be more useable.

Bleeding Dyes and Faded Fabrics

The Sarah's Choice block on the left shows serious bleeding. Not only did the blue fabric bleed, it migrated onto the background fabric, and now the blue fabric looks washed out or faded. Once this happens, the block is generally unusable, unless you are able to replace the bleeding fabrics before they ruin nearby fabrics. The Wheel of Fortune block on the right shows fading in the brown and pink fabrics. Fabrics often fade due to exposure to sunlight. Fading is bothersome, but useable. However, additional fading could occur so replacing faded fabrics with color fast fabrics is a good idea.

Grandmother's Flower Garden circa 1930

Nine Patch circa 1970

Monkey Wrench circa 1940

clean the blocks

The cleaning process is basically the same for both antique and modern blocks. However, antique blocks can be more challenging and time consuming. It is important to realize that at any time during the cleaning process, a block might tear, fade or even disintegrate, so extra care must be taken. If you cannot bear the thought of that happening with your blocks, do not attempt cleaning; contact a conservator or textile professional for advice.

Why Clean?

Even a block that looks clean may be dusty or lightly soiled. If you doubt my words, wash a quilt block that appears to be clean, and you will be amazed at how bright the colors are after cleaning. Over time, dust and grime can weaken the fibers of fabric, causing wear or even disintegration. If a quilt block is not fragile or otherwise unstable, a gentle cleaning will help to preserve the piece. It's always a good idea to test each fabric in the block by rubbing a dampened cotton swab or cloth on it before submerging an entire orphan block into water. This way, you can check for colorfastness before the colors begin to bleed. If there is a question about the best cleaning methods for any block, consult a professional.

Types of Stains

Cleaning does not always remove all stains from blocks. You may encounter:

• Cosmetic stains are unappealing but do not damage the fabric. Brown age spots or water spots are examples of cosmetic stains.

• Damaging stains have either already caused damage to fabrics or may do so in the future. Stains that contribute to fabric damage include mildew, dye migration, pet or animal urine.

If you've tried a basic washing but a stain is still present, it doesn't necessarily render the block unusable.

Options for Cosmetic (Non-Damaging) Stains

• If you can live with the stain, proceed with your quilt project.

❖ *materials* list

Disposable gloves

Color fixative

Gentle, nonphosphate quilt cleaner such as Orvus or QuiltCare

Plastic tub or sink (white or light-colored so that any bleeding of colors will be immediately apparent)

Spring water, if local water supply is hard or chemically treated

White paper towels

- If a non-damaging stain still bothers you, you to remove the stain with appropriately-gentle methods as directed on below.

Options for Damaging Stains

If the stain has weakened or damaged the fabrics around it, you should either:

- Replace the stained fabrics with something similar (see page 18)

- Do not use the block. (Instead, save its good pieces for replacing damaged fabrics in other blocks.)

Using Harsh Cleaners

Some stains and tough soils may not come out with the washing method detailed below. However, harsh cleaners can cause colors to fade or bleed and can even make some fabrics disintegrate. If a stained block will be unusable unless cleaned, and if you can live with the possibility of ruining it, you can try:

• Oxygenated cleanser or chlorine-free bleach.
Yes, even this type of cleanser can cause bleeding, fading or other damage to fabrics.

• Chlorine bleach. Use as a last resort on muslin or white background fabrics only.

✥ *cleaning* quilt blocks

1 Treat With Color Fixative

Before cleaning a block, test all fabrics for colorfastness by rubbing with a damp white cloth. Even if there is no color transference to the white cloth, that doesn't mean that the fabrics won't bleed during the cleaning process.

If there is any chance that the fabrics will bleed, whether the quilt block is new or old, treat it with a color fixative. Most likely, you won't know until too late whether the fabrics will bleed, so treat the blocks with a color fixative before washing. I have had reds, blues, blacks, and even pinks bleed during washing. When used correctly, a color fixative will set the dyes in the fabrics. To ensure the best results, carefully read and follow all product instructions.

If a fabric still bleeds after treatment with a color fixative, consider replacing the fabric (page 18) or not using the block at all.

2 Wet the Blocks With Plain Water

Prepare a clean light-colored tub or sink with warm but not hot water (use bottled spring water if your water is hard or treated with chemicals). Put block in the water. If cleaning many blocks at the same time, place a few blocks together in the water that have similar fabrics/colors.

Gently swish the blocks around in the water with your hands, taking care not to put any stress on the blocks because wet blocks are more fragile. Watch carefully for any bleeding of colors. If you see any dye in the water, remove the blocks immediately, rinse thoroughly in cold water and allow to dry flat. Before continuing, decide if you can replace the bleeding fabrics or if the block is completely unusable.

3 Wash With Gentle, Non-Phosphate Cleanser

If blocks did not bleed in step 2, add a gentle non-phosphate cleanser such as Orvus or Quiltcare, following the manufacturer's directions.

If the water becomes very dirty, remove the blocks from the water, lay them flat on a white towel or stack of plain white paper towels. Dump out the soiled water, rinse the tub, and wash the blocks again. Blocks that are heavily soiled and/or smelly may need to be washed several times. Each time that you wash the blocks, watch for fabric bleeding.

4 Rinse, Then Lay Flat Until Almost Dry

When the water remains clear, remove your blocks from the tub and place them in another tub of rinse water. Swish the blocks gently around with your hands. Do this several times with fresh water until you are positive that all of the cleanser is rinsed out. Lay the blocks flat on a stack of plain white paper towels and allow to dry until slightly damp.

5 Press

Heat an iron to the appropriate temperature for the fabric content. While blocks are slightly damp, press them carefully, taking care not to stretch or distort the quilt block. 'Pressing' is simply that—lifting the iron and putting it down. 'Ironing' is rubbing the iron around the fabric, which can could result in distortion and even damage. Press the front and the back of blocks, pressing seams in a way that avoids as much bulk as possible.

Squares and Stripes circa 2007

Nine Patch circa 1945

Twenty-Five Patch circa 1940

Replacing a Damaged Piece

Whether because of stains, faded fabrics, poor-quality fabrics, bleeding, holes, tears or fraying, sometimes your only option is to replace the damaged piece or pieces.

1. Find a suitable fabric for the missing piece. (See page 19.)

2. Take the block apart using a seam ripper. Carefully rip every couple of stitches, making sure not to catch any fabric with the ripper, and remove the thread instead of pulling the fabrics apart.

3. Using the original piece as a pattern, cut out the new piece.

4. Reassemble the block, sewing on the original seam lines.

5. Press.

making repairs

Orphaned blocks with weak seams, fraying or damaged pieces are salvageable. With a little love and attention, these can be fixed. However, only make repairs to a block *after* you've cleaned it. If a block can't hold up to the washing process, you really don't want to find out *after* making painstaking repairs.

Weak Seams

• If the seams are coming apart and the fabrics are sturdy, carefully sew on the original seam lines to reinforce the seams.

• In the case of insufficient seam allowances (less than ¼"), either sew over the original seam lines to reinforce the seams or take the block apart and resew, using an adequate seam allowance. Keep in mind that increasing the existing seam allowance will result in a smaller block.

Frayed Blocks

There are several options for fraying blocks:

1. If the fabric is frayed on the back of the block (in the seam allowance) only, check the seams for strength by tugging on the block.

• If the seams come apart, then you could take the block apart, recut the pieces smaller, and then sew it back together again.

• If the seams hold, then snip away the hanging threads carefully and continue with your project. To reinforce the seams, you might want to sew over the original seam lines.

2. If the edges of the block are only slightly frayed and won't compromise the ¼" seam allowance around the outside of the block, continue with your quilt project.

3. If the edges are badly frayed, either consider the block unusable or take the block apart, re-cut all block pieces to a uniform smaller size, thereby removing all of the fraying, and sew the block back together. The block will be smaller.

companion fabrics & blocks

Working with orphan quilt blocks is fun, especially when you are hunting for just the right companion fabrics or quilt blocks. This might be the reason you were waiting for to visit your local quilt shop or stop at the closest antique shop or flea market. While you are travelling, you might even find a garage sale or two to stop at.

Companion Fabrics

When working with orphan quilt blocks, particularly antique ones, it is important to have access to companion fabrics, either antique, vintage or modern reproductions. Finding and purchasing period fabrics can be a very time consuming and expensive project, but it is doable if that is your interest. There are numerous books written on the topic that can guide you.

Over the years, I have been able to collect antique vintage fabrics from many different sources—often the same places that I buy orphan blocks—garage sales, antique shops/shows/malls, flea markets, etc. I haven't necessarily sought out antique and vintage fabrics specifically, but I buy them when I find them. I don't usually use vintage and antique fabrics for borders, backings or bindings, but I do use them for repairing damaged blocks or even making additional blocks for a project.

As a quilter, I prefer to use 100% cotton fabric of good quality. Sometimes, however, the blocks and tops that I acquire may possess fabrics with fiber contents other than cotton. Many quilting trends of the past led to quilts with fabrics of different fiber contents. Take the crazy quilts from the late 1800s into the early 1900s, for example. They might contain silk, wool, velvet, cotton or linen. Additionally, good quality cotton fabrics were not always available, and quilters had to use what they could find.

What this means is that when you are rescuing orphan blocks, be prepared to use fabrics that match the blocks, whether you use antique fabrics, new reproductions, contemporary, or retro polyester fabrics.

Here is one more thought on companion fabrics—after you've gathered your blocks and have even settled on a wonderful design to make them shine, and you are auditioning fabrics, you might find the right fabrics in unusual places (or in this case time periods). Part of the fun of working with orphan blocks are the little surprises along the way!

Take the CRISS CROSS quilt, for example. The blocks themselves are circa 1890. The mauve companion fabric is a modern linen-look solid cotton, and the black is a modern marbled. Now, the striped border is what makes the quilt interesting—it's an 1830s reproduction. Wait, what? 1890s blocks with 1830s repro fabric? Take a minute and look, really look, at the quilt (page 44). The fabrics all work together. In fact, they all *like* each other. They don't care about eras and historic fabric trends. Sounds like a friendship crafted in heaven, doesn't it?

Companion Blocks

You might need to make a few "extra" quilt blocks to match existing orphans in order to have enough for a particular project. When I designed FAN FARE (page 110), the setting I chose had sixteen fan blocks, and I only had fifteen! Since I had the original quilter's scrapbag (or at least some of it), I searched out scraps that blended with the original fans. If you don't have access to vintage and antique fabrics, modern reproductions can also blend with your blocks.

Alternatively, you might choose to make new companion blocks to mix with your orphans. They could be the same design or different—it really depends on your vision and what your orphans require. I prefer to use very simple companion blocks with my orphan blocks because I do not want the companion blocks to overshadow the orphans—it's the orphan blocks' chance to shine.

19

Unequal Four Patch circa 1925

Nine Patch circa 1920

Unequal Four Patch circa 1925

common design
challenges & solutions

Here are some situations commonly encountered when working with orphan blocks, along with suggested solutions:

Challenge 1: Your blocks are smaller than those featured in the project you want to make.

Solution:

Add a border around all of your blocks and square them all to the correct size.

Challenge 2: Blocks appear to be the same size, but when you measure them individually, you find slight but significant size variations.

Solutions:

• Add a narrow border around the sides of the smaller blocks to make them the correct size.

• Trim down larger blocks to match the dimensions of smaller blocks.

• If the fabrics are cotton, you can stretch the smaller ones to make them a little larger, taking advantage of cotton's natural "give." Wet down the smaller blocks, stretch them gently but firmly to the correct dimensions and then pin all sides so that it can't shrink back to its original size as it dries. This is called blocking. (You can even block a whole quilt if you need to.)

• If all else fails, carefully take apart the larger blocks and resew with a slightly larger seam allowance so they match the size of the smaller blocks.

Challenge 3: You don't have enough of a certain block to make the project you want to.

Solutions:

• Go ahead—mix different blocks together, use a large square of coordinating fabric or piece new companion blocks. You are only limited by your own creativity.

• If you are determined to create companion blocks using matching or similar vintage or antique fabrics, like I did in the FAN FARE quilt, there are many sources available to you. If you don't have the original quilter's scrap bag, the best place to look is on the Internet, where you will find dealers who specialize in textiles. Some dealers can even find exact fabrics.

Challenge 4: Your blocks are too big for the project you are interested in.

Solutions:

• Enlarge the design to fit your blocks. This approach will require some careful planning.

• Separate larger blocks into smaller segments. Some blocks are made of smaller units sewn together (see the unequal Four Patch blocks at left). In these particular blocks, the large blocks can be taken apart to each yield four smaller units.

• Depending on how brave you are, you can trim the blocks down to the size that you need for the project. Keep in mind that you will lose seam allowances with this method.

Challenge 5: Your blocks have bias edges and are distorted.

Solutions:

This is a challenging problem with no single easy fix. It all depends on the blocks and what you are willing to do to them. Options include:

• Press or block the piece back into shape, if the fabrics can be ironed safely and if they are only slightly distorted.

• If distortion is severe, you might have to take the blocks apart, re-cut the fabrics and then sew them back together. This could result in smaller blocks than the originals.

• If you're comfortable taking a chance, you might be able to cut all the blocks to make them square and the same size. Not everyone feels comfortable about doing this, though. The problem with cutting blocks down is that you lose original seam allowances (if there were seam allowances to begin with) and will cut off triangle points, and squares/rectangles will not necessarily be square or rectangular. This really doesn't bother me—the blocks weren't perfectly pieced to begin with. The orphans don't complain, either; they just want to be loved and have a permanent home in a completed quilt.

• Depending on your method for working with distorted blocks and the fabric content, you might consider backing the blocks with a lightweight fusible interfacing to stop future stretching as you work with the blocks.

Challenge 6: You only have a few orphan blocks.

Solutions:

This is not a challenge, but an opportunity! If you have only a few blocks, try a table runner or small wall quilt. A single block could become a center medallion in a large quilt, or a one-of-a-kind evening bag. You could re-create blocks (see page 19), though working with what you have is often the best course of action. There are many settings in the following pages that show off the blocks in different ways. You'll find the home that your orphan blocks are looking for!

Sweet Solutions

The pretty blocks that are part of LAVENDER GREEN presented me with challenge 2—blocks that appeared the same size were actually different. So I added lavender borders to the smaller blocks to make them all a uniform size.

LAVENDER GREEN

page 86

finishing

Once you've inspected your blocks, cleaned and repaired them, and stitched them into the perfect setting, you now need to complete your project. Don't let former orphan quilt blocks turn into future UFOs.

Choosing and Preparing Backing Fabric

Selecting backing fabric is very much a personal choice. Keep in mind that a busy fabric will hide quilting stitches on the back of a quilt while a solid or near-solid fabric will make stitches more prominent, particularly if the thread on the back does not match the backing fabric choice.

Depending on the size of the quilt, you may need to sew 42-44" wide pieces of fabric together to get the desired dimensions. Or, you could try using wide quilt back fabrics, which are available at your local quilt shop. Just make sure to leave at least two to three extra inches of backing and batting all the way around the edges of the quilt top.

Layering

Press the entire quilt top carefully. Also press the backing fabric. Layer backing, batting, and quilt top. Pin or baste layers together. I try to avoid pinning or basting through old quilt blocks in order to avoid causing any damage. The batting and backing should extend beyond the edges of the quilt top by two to three inches on all sides. You are ready to quilt—but by hand? Or machine?

Quilting

Every quilter has his or her own idea about quilting, but the most basic decision you must make is between hand quilting and machine quilting. There is no right answer here, only personal preference. Hand and machine quilting each require certain skills and tools. If you want to quilt your project yourself but aren't sure you have the required skills or knowledge, take a hand or machine quilting class at your local quilt shop.

Whether you decide to hand quilt or machine quilt, you will need to select thread for quilting. I prefer 100% cotton thread; however, it is important to remember to match the thread to the fabrics, so if you are quilting polyester or poly cotton blocks, you will need to use a polyester or poly cotton thread.

Virginia Worm Fence circa 1925

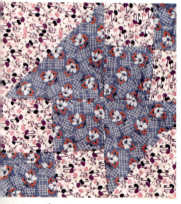

Hour Glass circa 1940

Hour Glass circa 1940

Attaching a Label

Your quilt is not complete without the addition of a label. A label should contain basic information such as who made the quilt, who the recipient is and a date of completion. Other information could include: a location, name of the quilt and the story of the quilt, or even a photo printed onto fabric.

When making a label, make sure to leave enough room to turn all four edges under. Sew the label to the back of the quilt.

If you aren't up to quilting it yourself, there are professional hand and machine quilters. Check with your local shop or guild to find professionals in your area. Make sure you see samples of the quilter's work before giving him or her your quilt, though. In a sample, look for even stitches, no tucks or puckers, balanced stitching on the front and back (you shouldn't see the top thread on the back or the bottom thread on the front), and a quilt design that compliments the quilt and does not compete or overpower it.

Pressing and Squaring Up

Once the quilting is completed, carefully press the entire quilt. Next, square up your quilt. In order to do this, you will need a large square acrylic ruler, a long rectangular ruler, a rotary cutter and a large cutting mat.

1. Place the square ruler in a corner of the quilt.

2. Line up the square with the seam lines (using the ruler lines), not the outer edge of the quilt.

3. Take note of the measurement lines on the ruler. Are both sides of the seam lines on the same ruler lines (say, 4 ½")? If not, manipulate the ruler some more until your corner is truly square.

4. When you are positive that the corner is square, carefully cut off any extra fabric beyond the outer edge of the ruler.

5. Repeat this with all four corners.

6. Once the corners are squared, use a long rectangular ruler to connect the squared corners together and cut off any extra fabric on all sides of the quilt. Be careful not to let the ruler slip or your quilt will not be square.

A final check to make sure your quilt is square is to fold the quilt in half, carefully matching edges. Then fold it in half again, so the quilt is folded in fourths. All edges and the four corners will line up if the quilt is truly square.

If the edges and corners do not match up, you may need to square up the quilt again. Take care to only trim slivers of fabric away.

Binding

When the quilting is done and the quilt is squared up, it's time to add binding. Throughout history, there have been many different methods of finishing the edges of quilts. If you are replicating an antique quilt and want to use authentic binding, a little research into the era will yield the techniques of the time.

1. Cut binding strips 2¼" by the width of fabric. Sew ends of strips together to make one continuous strip of binding.

2. Fold and press binding strip in half lengthwise, wrong sides together.

3. Align the raw edge of the binding to the raw edge of the quilt on the lower right side. Start sewing the binding to the quilt eight to ten inches from the beginning of the binding strip (figure 3). It's helpful to place a pin where the binding strip begins.

4. When you get to a corner, stop sewing ¼" from the edge and backstitch two or three stitches. Cut threads. Fold the binding strip at a 45 degree angle away from the quilt (figure 1), then fold the strip over (figure 2), aligning the raw edges on the next side of the quilt (figure 3).

5. Continue sewing the binding to the quilt in this way. Stop sewing three or four inches from the pin.

6. Cut the ending of binding strip 2¼" beyond the pin.

7. Remove the pin. Open both loose sections of binding. Match binding ends with right sides together at a 45 degree angle. Pin. Sew across ends.

8. Refold loose sections of binding with wrong sides together. Finish sewing raw edges of binding to raw edges of quilt.

9. Sew binding to back of quilt, taking care to miter corners smoothly.

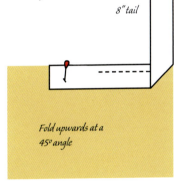

8" tail

Fold upwards at a 45° angle

Figure 1

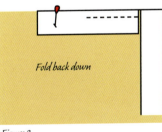

Fold back down

Figure 2

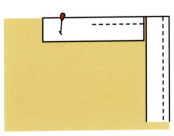

Figure 3

quilt projects

Now that you've located your own orphan quilt blocks, examined them, cleaned and repaired them, you are ready to select the perfect project to give your orphans the home they've always wanted. There are fourteen orphan block quilt projects to choose from, ranging from a single block table runner to a queen-sized quilt with several different collections of blocks. The projects are arranged chronologically beginning with orphan blocks circa 1880 and ending with orphan blocks circa 1955.

Your orphan blocks will help you to find the right setting to make them sparkle. Each project lists the number of blocks and block dimensions needed. If you find the ideal setting but you have a different number of blocks than the project calls for or the size of your blocks is different, consult the Common Designs Challenges and Solutions section (page 20).

Perhaps you fall in love with one of the projects and do not have antique or vintage orphan quilt blocks. Do not despair—at the end of most of the projects, there is a modern variation using contemporary quilt blocks! These variations will inspire you to complete that set of last year's unfinished sampler blocks or even to check out a quilt block reference and make new blocks. Of course, whether you use orphaned antique blocks or new contemporary blocks, a great part of the fun is finding just the right fabrics.

So, what are you waiting for? Turn the page.

Quilt block circa 1880

mad for madder

The five Four-X blocks in this quilt date from about 1880. The blocks all use the same combination of muslin and a madder-style fabric. Madder was a common vegetable dye in the 1800s. Depending on which metal salts were used in combination with the madder dye, different colors could be achieved—purples, pinks, reds, oranges and browns, including the ever-popular Turkey Red. When people think of quilts from the mid- to late 1800s, they often envision shades of brown; hence, the quilt name MAD FOR MADDER.

❖ *shopping* list

Orphan Blocks

Five 12" square finished size

Companion Fabrics

Background: 1¼ yards
Borders: Four colors, ⅜ yard each

To Finish

Batting: 64" × 64"
Backing fabric: 64" × 64"
Binding fabric: ¾ yard

✤ *design* considerations

When I purchased these blocks at an antique shop, they were mixed in with a group of newer blocks in the same pattern. The newer blocks, sadly, were stained and were not as well pieced as the older ones, so I chose to work with just the five older blocks. Designing a quilt around just five orphan blocks was a challenge, but I think you'll agree that the design is stunning in its simplicity.

For the companion fabrics, I selected a range of new madder-style reproduction fabrics, which are widely available today.

Make 8

 Cut eight 12½" squares from background fabric. Set four aside until step 6.

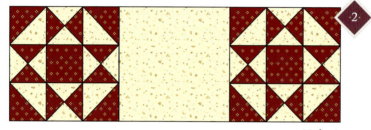

Make 2

Sew a background square in between two orphan quilt blocks. Make two identical rows. Press seam allowances toward background fabric.

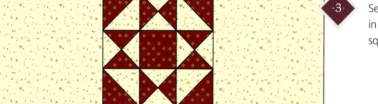

Make 1

Sew an orphan quilt block in between two background squares.

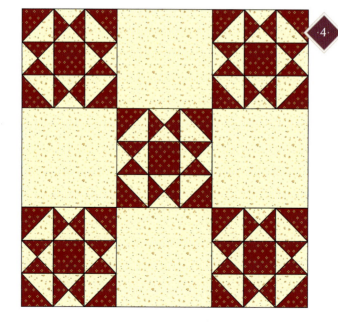

Sew rows together, following diagram.

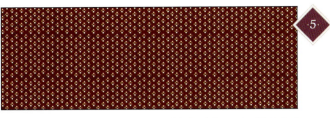

Make 4 (assorted fabrics)

◆5◆ From each of the four assorted border fabrics, cut a 12½" by 36½" strip.

◆6◆ To the end of each border strip, sew a background square (set aside from step 1).

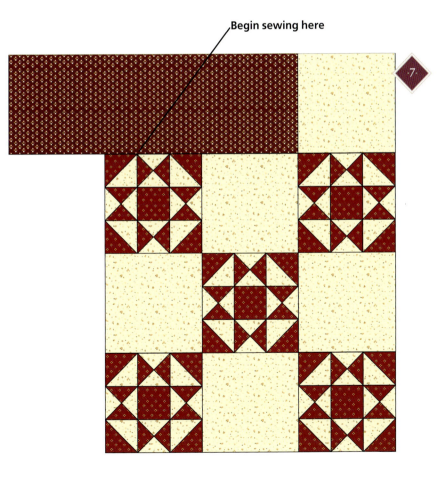

Begin sewing here

◆7◆ Sew one of the border units from step 6 to top of quilt center. Matching the right edges of the border unit and the quilt center, begin sewing approximately 16" from the left side of border (note that the border will overhang the quilt center on the left). This will ensure that the borders go on in a pinwheel fashion—you will complete this seam at the end. Press the seam towards the border before continuing.

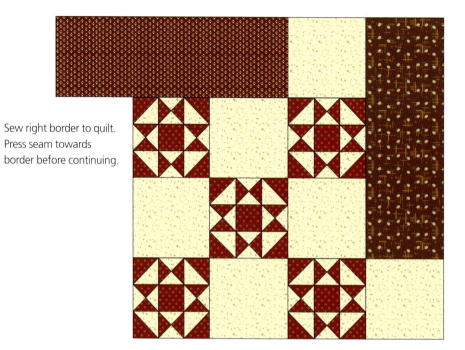

·8· Sew right border to quilt. Press seam towards border before continuing.

·9· Sew bottom border to quilt. Press seam towards border before continuing.

Pin unsewn top border section out of the way and sew left side border to quilt. Press seam towards border before continuing.

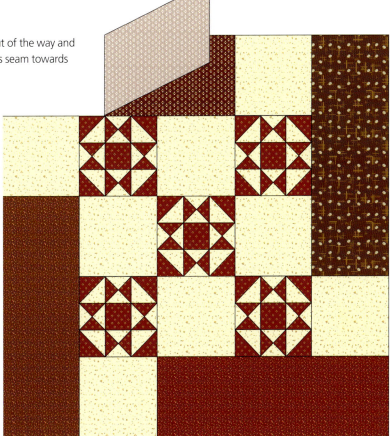

 Unpin the unsewn top border and fold it right sides together with the quilt. Carefully align the raw edge of the unsewn section with the quilt and left border. Pin and sew remaining top border section to quilt. Press the seam toward the border.

Finish the quilt as desired (see pages 22-23).

Mad for Madder

60" × 60"

Four-X blocks found at an antique shop

Pieced by the author

Machine-quilted by Gaynel Sickles

❖ modern *variation*

STRAWBERRY FIZZ is the same basic design as MAD FOR MADDER except that the background squares are framed squares instead of plain and the border fabric is the same instead of four assorted fabrics. The framed square blocks add a lot of drama and graphic appeal to the variation quilt. The fabrics in MAD FOR MADDER are all very harmonious while the fabrics in STRAWBERRY FIZZ vary in intensity, causing a lot of movement. Isn't it amazing that the same setting can yield a very traditional nineteenth century-looking quilt and a hip contemporary quilt?

Strawberry Fizz

60" × 60"

Pieced by Leslie Lattner

Machine-quilted by the author

Quilt block circa 1880

flying pinwheels

These Double Pinwheel blocks, circa 1880, were part of that inspiring first collection of tops and blocks I purchased at a local garage sale. Louetta Hoffman, the remarkable woman who inspired me to make orphan block quilts, had these as part of her collection. Since Louetta was born in 1897, these blocks must have had another maker. Perhaps she collected orphaned blocks herself! Read more about Louetta on page 42.

❖ *shopping* list

Orphan Blocks

Ten 8" (finished size)

Companion Fabrics

60 scraps of light-colored fabrics, each at least 2½" × 5". From these, cut 60 pairs of 2½" × 2½" squares for Flying Geese (120 total)

60 scraps of medium to dark fabrics, each at least 2½" × 4½". From these, cut 60 2½" × 4½" rectangles for Flying Geese

¼ yard dark fabric for sashing
¼ yard each of two medium or dark fabrics for borders

To Finish

Batting: 42" × 50"
Backing fabric: 42" × 50"
Binding fabric: ⅜ yard

❖ *design* considerations

I can understand why these blocks remained orphans. They were not very square, the triangle points were not sharp, and the seams were wiggly. Despite those flaws, these are some of my favorite blocks because of their simple, sweet charm.

The flying geese setting seemed to be just right to showcase these great blocks. Knowing that vertical placement of blocks separated by strips was a common practice in the nineteenth century and that flying geese quilts were popular in the latter half of the 1800s led me to design this particular setting.

Sew five of the orphan blocks (8" finished size) end to end to create a strip of blocks. Repeat to make a second strip. Press seam allowances to either direction.

Make 2

Make 2

Measure the two block strips and cut four strips of sashing fabric, each strip 1½" wide by the length of the block strip (ideally 40½"). Attach sashing strips to both sides of each block strip, matching centers and pinning as necessary.

On the wrong side of a background square, draw a diagonal line from the bottom left corner to the top right corner. Place the background square on one side of a medium/dark rectangle, right sides together, matching corners and outer edges. Sew on the drawn line. Trim both the medium/dark fabric and the background square ¼" above the sewing line.

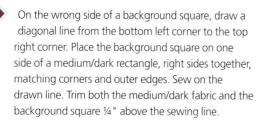

Trim away

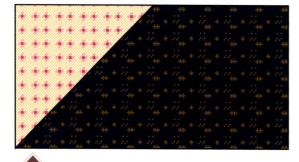

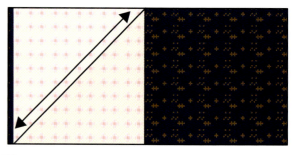

Make 60

Flip the triangle open and press.

Repeat steps 3 and 4 on the other side of the rectangle to finish one Flying Geese unit. Make a total of 60 assorted Flying Geese units.

Sew 20 Flying Geese units together to make a strip (ideal length 40½"). Repeat two more times for a total of three strips. If your blocks are not exactly 8" finished, you may need to adjust the number of Flying Geese units in your strips. For example, in Flying Pinwheels, I only needed 19 Flying Geese in each unit due to slight size differences.

·7·
Sew the three Flying Geese strips to the sides of the blocks with sashing strips following the diagram, reversing the direction of the center Flying Geese strip if desired.

·8·
Measure quilt through the center vertically. Cut two border strips from the first border fabric 2½" by the vertical measurement (ideally 40½"). Sew border strips to sides of quilt center, matching centers.

·9·
Measure quilt through the center horizontally. Cut two border strips from the second border fabric 2½" by this length (ideally 37½"). Sew borders to top and bottom of quilt, matching centers.

Finished as desired (see pages 22-23).

Flying Pinwheels

36" × 44"

Double Pinwheel blocks from the author's
Louetta Hoffman collection

Pieced and quilted by the author

❖ quiltmaker
Louetta Shoemaker Hoffman

In 2006, I saw an ad in the local newspaper about a nearby garage sale that included "vintage quilt squares and fabric" in its description. My mother and I were the first ones there and suddenly, I was the owner of a large collection of antique and vintage quilt blocks and fabric. I was ecstatic! As I paid for my wonderful treasures, I asked the woman about the collection. She explained that the quilt items had belonged to her grandmother, Louetta Hoffman. I went back the next day and bought another stack of quilt tops, blocks and fabric. Louetta's granddaughter, Nancy, and I stayed in touch, and I added more of her items to my collection over the next few years.

Born 10 October 1897, Louetta Shoemaker was the daughter of German immigrants, raised on a farm in rural Pennsylvania. She married and went from her family's home to live with her husband, Walter Jacob Hoffman. She fed her chickens out the back kitchen door, slopped the hogs, tended her vegetable garden and nurtured flowers to grow everywhere. Louetta also made quilts—lots and lots of quilts. Little is known about Louetta's early life, but she probably learned to sew at a young age from her mother or grandmother. There were a lot of Four Patch and Nine Patch blocks from around 1900-1910 in the collection. I can imagine a young Louetta carefully selecting bits and pieces from her mother's scrap bag and then painstakingly stitching the small squares together into quilt patches as she learned to make neat straight stitches.

Louetta was more than just a quilter, though. The collection of quilt tops, blocks and fabrics that I acquired spanned more than a hundred years from the 1840s to the 1960s. Some of the pieces actually predated Louetta! We can only speculate that they might have been made by her mother

Wedding photo of Louetta Shoemaker and Walter Hoffman, circa 1915. Photo courtesy of Nancy Nyilyk.

and/or grandmother. Louetta's granddaughter believed that Louetta did quilting for other people who might have given her their orphan blocks and tops. So, Louetta was not only a quilter, she was also a collector.

Louetta passed away on 30 January 1981, at the age of 88.

Then, in 2006, I stumbled across that amazing collection of orphan blocks, fabric and unfinished quilt tops. Louetta's pieces spoke to me, and I knew I had to do something with them. Although she died when I was just a child and I never had the opportunity to meet her, her unfinished work inspired me. She lives on through the memories of her loved ones, her completed quilts and her pieces yet to be completed.

Quilt block circa 1890

criss cross

Adear friend, Marsha, knowing my love of old orphan blocks, asked me several years ago if she could give me her collection of antique blocks, purchased at local garage and rummage sales, because no one in her family was interested in them. I, of course, agreed. Then, at our guild Christmas party in 2008, there was an extra gift for me. I opened the box and to my surprise, there were several collections of antique blocks, including these 1890s Cross Roads blocks. Thanks, Marsha!

❖ *shopping* list

Orphan Blocks

Five 12" (finished size) blocks (it's okay if one of the five is slightly smaller)

Companion Fabrics

Fabric A (lighter): 1¼ yards
Fabric B (darker): 1¼ yards
Border: 1¾ yards

To Finish

Batting: 60" × 60"
Backing fabric: 60" × 60"
Binding fabric: ½ yard

✤ *design* considerations

I spent quite a bit of time deciding which blocks from the set to use. I finally settled on the four matching blocks and the single center block because they were different from the other blocks in the set. These blocks gave me a lot of problems because they were made from a thinner fabric and the outer edges were all biases. Looking back, I should have used a light interfacing on the backs of the blocks to stabilize them (one of the solutions offered on page 21, Common Design Challenges and Solutions), but when I realized what was happening, I was already too far into the project to do that. Despite the problems, I feel that the quilt is quite breathtaking.

·1· From fabric A, cut two 9" strips. From these strips, use a long ruler with a 45 degree angle to subcut four 12½" diamonds, following the diagram. Repeat using fabric B.

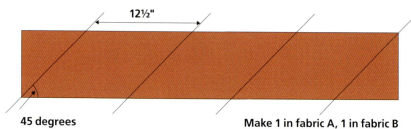

12½"

45 degrees

Make 1 in fabric A, 1 in fabric B

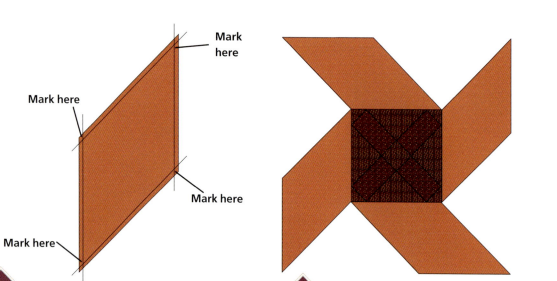

Mark here

Mark here

Mark here

Mark here

·2· Because you will be sewing set-in seams, mark ¼" seam allowances on all corners/points of the diamonds on the wrong side of the fabric. When you are sewing these pieces, do not sew into the seam allowance. This will ensure that the pieces fit together properly.

·3· Measure the orphan quilt blocks and choose the smallest one for the center block of the quilt. Sew the fabric A diamonds to the sides of the center quilt block in a counterclockwise manner, stopping and backstitching to lock the seam at the marked seam allowances.

·4· Paying close attention to the marked seam allowances, set in the remaining four orphan blocks. Setting-in quilt blocks is like fitting a puzzle piece inside of a puzzle. Take your time and remember not to sew into the seam allowances. Backstitch at the ends to lock your stitches.

·5· Set in a fabric B diamond between each quilt block and fabric A diamond.

Make 4

·6· Cut an 18½" square from fabric A. Repeat using fabric B. Cut the two squares on both diagonals to yield four triangles of each fabric.

Sew a fabric A triangle to a fabric B triangle. Repeat three more times, yielding four triangle sets.

·7· Sew triangle sets to corners of quilt.

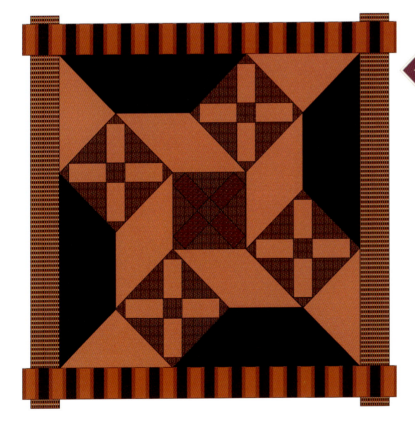

·8· Measure your quilt through the center both horizontally and vertically (ideally it will be 46½" × 46½"). Cut four strips of border fabric, each measuring 4½" wide by the above measurement plus 12". (If you cut the borders from the length of the fabric, there is no need to piece strips together. This technique works particularly well with striped borders, which can be difficult to piece.)

You will be making mitered corners on the border. To do so, mark the wrong side of the borders ¼" in from each corner of the quilt. Matching centers, sew border strips to top and bottom edges of quilt, then to left and right sides, stopping at the ¼" corner marks. The border strips will meet at the ¼" seam allowance marks and there will be excess fabric. Do not cut away the excess fabric.

·9· Fold the quilt in half diagonally, right sides together, to line up the border strips. Draw a 45 degree diagonal line from the ¼" mark where the borders meet to the outer edge of the border. Pin and sew seam on line, beginning at outside edge and sewing towards the ¼" mark. Once sewn, look at front side to make sure the miter is accurate, and then cut away the excess fabric ¼" beyond diagonal seam.

Repeat for the other three corners. Press seams toward the border.

Sewing line

Quilt, folded diagonally

Sewing line

Criss Cross

54" × 54"

Cross Roads blocks from the collection of Marsha Waite

Pieced by the author

Machine-quilted by Gaynel Sickles

❖ modern *variation*

Sometimes, quilters work from the outside in, as I did here with LAGOON. Although I already had the setting, my design decisions began with the border fabric. I chose the bright blue border with a bold pattern, and added a second, smaller interior border in a darker color. This led me to deciding to use four matching Four X variation blocks—in bright blue and rich brown—and a framed square for the center. I also changed the arrangement of the diamonds in the variation. In CRISS CROSS, the contrasting light and dark diamonds really ground the orphan quilt blocks. Here, the contrast isn't as intense, which allows the Four X blocks to float, even seem to move, around the center.

Lagoon

56" x 56"

Pieced and machine-quilted by the author

45

indigo delight

This quilt uses a single Papa's Delight block in the center, accompanied by four Nine Patch blocks, all circa 1900. The Papa's Delight block was part of my Louetta Hoffman collection while the Nine Patch blocks probably came out of an auction box many years before. Orphan quilt blocks from different places, made by different people, but they came together in one quilt. I named this quilt INDIGO DELIGHT in reference to the Papa's Delight block and the indigo blue fabrics.

Indigo and white quilts were very popular at the end of the 1800s. Indigo was a very stable dye and stood up to repeated washings, but interestingly enough, a lot of "best" quilts were made in indigo and white and survive today. Additionally, it is fascinating to note that the colors of the organization, The Women's Christian Temperance Union (WCTU), were also blue and white. I wonder…

❖ *shopping* list

Orphan Blocks

One 12" (finished size) block for center
Four 9" (finished size) companion blocks

Companion Fabrics

Background for quilt center: ⅝ yard
First border: ⅜ yard
Outer border: ⅝ yard

To Finish

Batting: 48" × 48"
Backing fabric: 48" × 48"
Binding fabric: ½ yard

❖ *design* considerations

The lone Papa's Delight block is an eye-catching block with interesting gently curved pieces. I knew I had to create a quilt around it, even if there was only one block. This created a challenge, but I found four similar-age Nine Patch blocks in the same color scheme, so a nine patch setting emerged with the Papa's Delight block as the centerpiece. Another dilemma popped up when I discovered that the Nine Patch blocks were smaller than the Papa's Delight block. I solved this by making the four background blocks into rectangles instead of the usual squares.

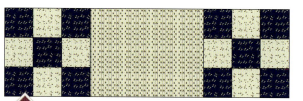

Cut 4

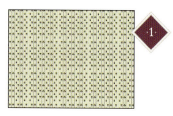 Cut two strips from the background fabric, 9½" by the width of the fabric. From these two strips, subcut a total of four 9½" × 12½" segments. (If using a striped fabric, as I did, pay attention to the direction of your stripes.)

Make 2

 Sew one background rectangle between two 9½" companion blocks. Press seam allowances toward background rectangles in all steps.

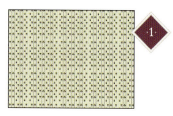 Sew the 12½" block between two background rectangles.

 Sew units together following the diagram.

·5· Measure your quilt through the center vertically. Cut two inner border strips 2½" by this length (ideally 30½") and sew to sides of quilt, matching centers.

·6· Measure your quilt through the center horizontally. Cut two inner border strips 2½" wide by this length (ideally 34½") and sew to top and bottom of quilt, matching centers.

·7· Measure your quilt through the center vertically. Cut two outer border strips 4½" wide by this length (ideally 34½") and sew to sides of quilt, matching centers.

·8· Measure your quilt through the center horizontally. Cut two outer border strips 4½" wide by this length (ideally 42½"), piecing as needed. Sew to top and bottom of quilt, matching centers.

Finish as desired (see pages 22-23).

Indigo Delight

42" × 42"

Papa's Delight block from author's
Louetta Hoffman collection; Nine
Patch blocks from an auction

Pieced and machine-quilted by the author

❖ modern *variation*

I had always wanted to create a quilt using Mariner's Compass blocks, but was always a little bit too nervous to try it. I finally worked up the courage and made a single Mariner's Compass block. It wasn't perfect, but I felt triumphant because I'd tried something new.

This modern variation, MATEYS, evolved from the Compass block in the center, much like INDIGO DELIGHT developed from the Papa's Delight block. The Mariner's Compass block made me think of the ocean, which naturally led me to think of pirates. I found the delightful bear pirate stripe fabric and instantly saw it in the background rectangles with an ocean wave border. Using a novelty stripe fabric in place of a shirting-type fabric really changed the look.

Mateys

41" × 41"

Pieced and machine-quilted by the author

bows & patches
table runner

These circa 1900 Bow Tie and Four Patch blocks also came from different sources, but they look like they've been together forever. I purchased the bow tie blocks at an annual quilt show that I attend at the Chautauqua Institute in Chautauqua, New York. The Four Patch blocks came in a larger set of scrappy blocks purchased at an antique shop on the Institute grounds. The interesting thing is that I actually purchased the Four Patch blocks the year before I bought the bow tie blocks

❖ *shopping* list

Orphan Blocks

Three 9" (finished size) blocks
Four 4½" (finished size) blocks

To Finish

Batting: 19" × 44"
Backing fabric: 19" × 44"

❖ *design* considerations

There were seven Bow Tie blocks, but three of the blocks were sewn together one way while the other four were sewn in a different way. I spent some time arranging and rearranging the blocks, but didn't like the results. I had *almost* decided to separate and resew the three blocks so that the matched the others, but then decided to try something using the three different blocks in their own arrangement. Once I placed them on point, this table runner design was born. Adding the Four Patch blocks completed the design.

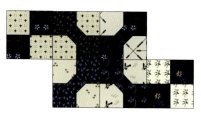

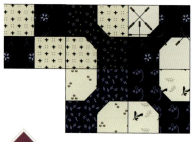

◆1◆ Sew one 4½" block to the bottom right side of one 9" block.

◆2◆ Sew one 4½" block to the top left side of a 9" block and one 4½" block to the bottom right side of the same block.

◆3◆ Sew the last 4½" block to the top left side of the final 9" block. Press seams toward small blocks.

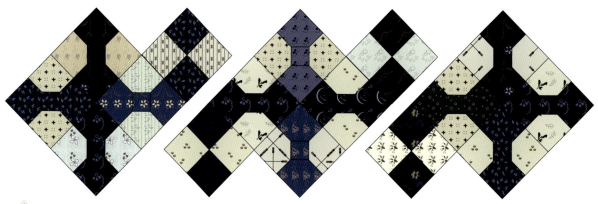

◆4◆ Arrange the blocks as shown and sew seams between the three block sections, taking care to match the side points of the 9" blocks together. Press carefully.

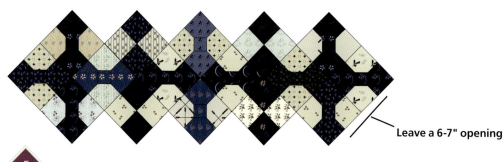

Leave a 6-7" opening

◆5◆ Due to its many points, this runner is finished envelope-style. Layer the runner top and backing fabric *right sides together* and place on top of batting. Pin through all layers. With the wrong side of the top facing up, sew around all sides using a ¼" seam allowance. Leave a 6" or 7" opening along one straight side at end. Cut the points and clip into the valleys just outside the stitching line to reduce bulk.

·6· Turn runner right side out through opening. Using a ball point bodkin or other rounded tool, carefully push all points right side out. Smooth runner out and press. Hand sew opening closed. Quilt as desired.

Bows & Patches

13" × 40" table runner

Bow Tie blocks purchased from a quilt show vendor; Four Patch blocks purchased from an antique shop

Runner pieced and machine-quilted by the author

❖ modern *variation*

The four contemporary blocks in ZIGZAG were left over from a project I made several years before. They were as modern as the Bow Tie blocks were traditional. I decided to see what would happen when I placed them in the BOWS & PATCHES setting. I put them on point and liked what I saw, but after trying out a few companion pieced blocks, I decided that the runner would be too busy. So I used a black-on-white print fabric to tone down the bright blocks. It is hard to see that the two runners actually use the same setting—the BOWS & PATCHES runner is one uniform piece with the blocks blending into each other, while ZIGZAG boldly shows off its individual blocks, separated by light squares. Both runners were finished envelope-style due to the many corners and points.

ZigZag

13" × 40" table runner

Runner pieced and machine-quilted by the author

Quilt block circa 1910

americana medallion

The central Eight Point String Star blocks, circa 1910, were part of my Louetta Hoffman collection. I was quite fascinated with these blocks because of the many fabrics seemingly rescued from clothing and household sewing projects. The bits and pieces were then sewed onto paper foundations, which were later removed when the diamond sections were pieced together into stars.

❖ *shopping* list

Orphan Blocks

Four 12" (finished size) blocks for center medallion

Four 5" (finished size) blocks for medallion setting triangles

Four 9" (finished size) blocks for outer border cornerstones, or 1 fat quarter

Companion Fabrics

Four Patch border: 1¼ yard total assorted fabrics, or 48 Four Patch blocks (4" finished size) and 8 half Four Patch blocks

Background: 2 yards

Medallion setting rectangles: ⅝ yard

Medallion setting triangle cornerstones: 1 fat quarter

Inner border: 1¾ yard

Inner border cornerstones: 1 fat quarter

Outer border: 2½ yards

To Finish

Batting: Double/queen-sized

Backing: 88" × 96"

Binding: 1 yard

✦ *design* considerations

When I first spied these blocks, I immediately thought they would be great as the center of a medallion quilt. I was thrilled to discover a total of ten blocks, but did not want to use them all in the same project. Knowing that I needed to make a large quilt, I chose a medallion setting using four of the blocks, with a series of surrounding borders. Once I sifted through my vintage and antique blocks, I came up with some small Eight Point Stars and stacks of Four Patch blocks, all from roughly the same time period and using similar fabrics.

As I worked on the setting for these blocks, I met a roadblock—I wanted to continue the eight point star design all the way to the outside borders, but I didn't have any star blocks in the right size. My solution—I made four Eight Point Star blocks using reproduction fabrics!

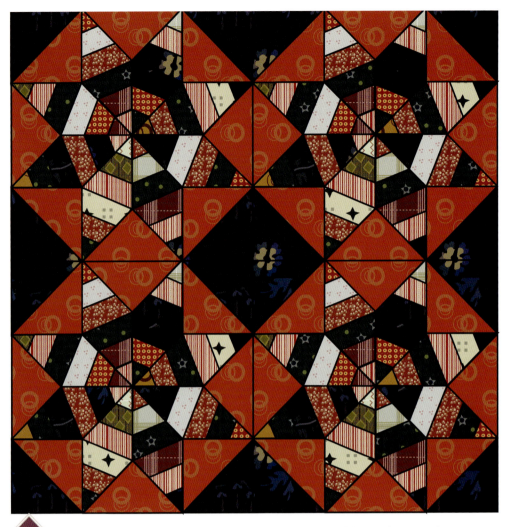

 ·1· Arrange the four blocks in a pleasing manner for the center medallion and sew together into two rows. Press. Join the rows.

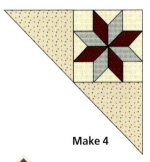

Make 4

Make 4

Make 4

 ·2· From the medallion setting rectangle fabric, cut four 5[7/8]" squares. Cut in half diagonally to yield eight triangles. Sew background triangles to sides of small orphan blocks. Press seam allowance toward triangle.

·3· From the background fabric, cut eight 5¾" × 10½" rectangles. Sew one rectangle to the side of each triangle unit. Press seam allowance toward rectangles.

 ·4· Cut four 5¾" squares from the medallion setting triangle cornerstone fabric. Sew a cornerstone to one end of the remaining setting rectangles from step 3. Press seam allowance toward rectangles.

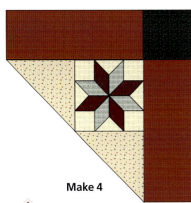 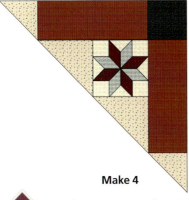

Make 4   **Make 4**

◆ 5 ◆ Sew the unit from step 4 to the top of each triangle unit. Press seam allowance toward rectangle.

◆ 6 ◆ Cut four 6⅛" squares from background fabric. Cut in half diagonally to yield eight triangles. Sew background triangles to corners of triangle units. Press seam allowances toward triangles.

◆ 7 ◆ Sew two triangle units to opposite edges of the center medallion, matching centers. The ends of the triangle units will extend beyond the edges of the center medallion. Do *not* trim excess fabric at this point.

Sew the remaining triangle units to the other two sides of the center medallion, matching centers. The center medallion will float inside the frame of the triangle units. Trim excess triangle points. Press seam allowance toward triangle units. At this point, the quilt ideally should measure 37½" square.

·8· Cut two 5" background fabric strips by 37½". Sew to sides of the medallion.

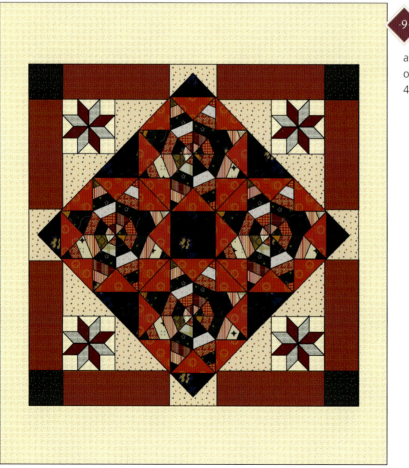

·9· Cut two 9" background fabric strips by 54½", pieced as needed. Sew to top and bottom of medallion. Quilt is now ideally 46½" × 54½".

Make 52   **Make 4**

·10· If you are using finished blocks for the Four Patch border, skip to step 11. Or, from the assorted fabrics, cut a total of 200 2½" squares. Sew squares together to make 48 whole Four Patch blocks and 4 half Four Patch blocks.

·11· Make a border strip by sewing together eleven whole Four Patch blocks and one half block. Make two. (Please note that depending on your quilt measurements, you may need to adjust the number of whole/half four patch units. If the Four Patch border does not match the length of the quilt center, you may need to ease in some fullness or increase/decrease seam allowances in the four patch units slightly until the border fits the quilt.)

Make 2

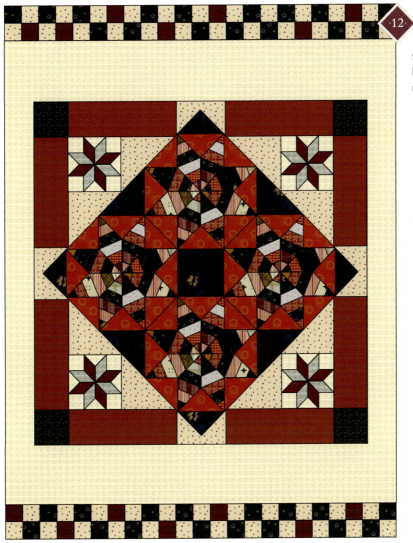

·12· Sew the Four Patch border strips to top and bottom of quilt, matching centers.

·13· Sew 13 whole Four Patch blocks together and one half block. Make two. Sew to sides of quilt. (Again, please note that depending on your quilt measurements, you may need to adjust the number of whole/half Four Patch units. If the Four Patch border does not match the length of the quilt center, you may need to ease in some fullness or increase/decrease seam allowances in the four patch units slightly until the border fits the quilt.)

·14· Measure your quilt vertically and horizontally through the center. Ideally, it should be 54½" × 62½". Cut four 6½" wide strips of inner border fabric (two strips by your best horizontal measurement and two strips by your best vertical measurement), piecing as needed. Sew the horizontally measured strips to top and bottom of the quilt. Set aside the vertical strips until step 15.

·15· Cut four 6½" squares from inner border cornerstone fat quarter. Sew
a square to each end of the vertically measured inner border strips and
sew to sides of quilt.

·16· Measure your quilt horizontally and vertically through the centers once again. Ideally, it should be 66½" × 74½". Cut four 9½" strips of outer border fabric (two strips by your best horizontal measurement and two strips by your best vertical measurement), piecing as needed. Sew the horizontally measured strips to top and bottom of quilt. Set aside the vertical strips until step 17.

·17· Cut four 9½" squares from outer border cornerstone fat quarter (or use four orphan blocks).
Sew a square (or orphan block) to each end of the vertically measured inner border strips and sew to the sides of quilt. Finish as desired (see pages 22-23).

Americana Medallion

84" × 92"

The four large String Star blocks were purchased at a garage sale (part of the Louetta Hoffman collection). The four small Eight Point Stars were purchased from a different garage sale. The Four Patch blocks in the border were purchased from an antique shop.

Pieced by the author

Machine-quilted by Cindy Beggs and Barb Shuck

red & black surprise

These seven Mosaic blocks were part of a larger set of blocks, circa 1910, given to me by fellow guild member, Alberta Kiss. Each block consisted of sixteen triangle squares sewn together in four rows across by four rows down. The triangle square is one of the most basic shapes in patchwork patterns.

❖ *shopping* list

Orphan Blocks

Seven 12" (finished size) blocks

Companion Fabrics

Pinwheel: ½ yard
Inner border: ½ yard

To Finish

Batting: 42" × 42" batting
Backing fabric: 1¼ yards
Binding fabric: ⅜ yard

❖ *design* considerations

This was an interesting set of blocks with many possibilities—there were lots of different fabric combinations, and many blocks even featured a variety of fabrics for the lights and the darks. I decided to challenge myself to do something different, something unexpected with them. So (gasp!), I cut the blocks up. I envisioned a pinwheel-type center surrounded by smaller block segments, sewn side to side. I cut two of the blocks diagonally through the center from corner to corner for the large pinwheel. I cut the other five blocks in half once, and then cut the halves in half for the outer border blocks.

Keep in mind that when working with chopped-up blocks, seam allowances are frequently lost due to the actual cutting (instead of ripping out the seams with a seam ripper, which would retain the original seam allowances). Points on triangles will be lost and squares and rectangles may be somewhat distorted as the new seam allowance includes parts of the block components. With that said, however, it was fun to experiment with a few simple blocks.

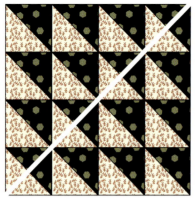 

Cut 4 triangles

Make 4 triangles

Make 4 blocks

 1 Select two orphan blocks for the center pinwheel. Cut each block once diagonally to yield four triangles.

2 From the pinwheel fabric, cut two 12½" squares. Cut each square in half diagonally, to yield four triangles.

 3 Sew an orphan block triangle to a pinwheel triangle along the diagonal.

4 Sew the four blocks together into a four patch pinwheel design, aligning same block triangles diagonally from each other. Press center seams open to reduce bulk.

5 Measure quilt through the center vertically. Cut two inner border strips 1½" by this length (ideally 23¼", but this measurement may be different if you cut the blocks versus separating at the seams) and sew to sides of quilt, matching centers. Press seam allowances toward border strips.

Measure the quilt through the center horizontally. Write this figure down; you will need it again in step 12.

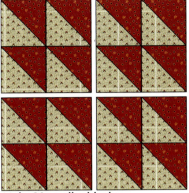

Make 20 smaller blocks

Make 4

·6· With the remaining five orphan blocks, cut or separate the seams of each block to make four smaller blocks, approximately 6½" × 6½" (if you are cutting the blocks apart, your blocks will be smaller).

·7· Sew four smaller orphan block segments together in a row. Make four rows. (In the project quilt, one of the four orphan blocks was used for each corner).

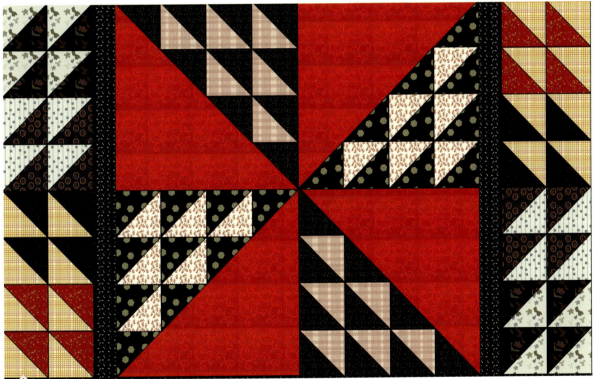

·8· Measure the small-block strips and compare these measurements to the length of the quilt.

• If the small block strips are longer than the quilt, you will need to take the seams of the strip in slightly until the strip fits the quilt.

• If the small block strips are shorter than the quilt, you can add narrow spacer strips of the inner border fabric to the ends of the block strips so that the strip fits the quilt.

• If the measurements are just slightly off, see if the shorter piece can be blocked (see Challenge 2, page 20) just a bit to make the pieces match. Be careful not to distort the strip by too much stretching.

Sew one small-block row to each side of the quilt.

·9· Measure quilt through the center horizontally. Cut two strips of inner border fabric 1½" wide by this measurement (ideally 35¾", but this measurement may be different if you cut the blocks versus separating at the seams) and sew to top and bottom of quilt, matching centers. Press seam allowances toward border strips.

Make 2

·10· Measure the height of the remaining small block strips and cut four 1½" wide × your measurement strips (ideally 6 ½") from the inner border fabric.

Review the horizontal measurement of the quilt from step 5 (before you added the small block strips) and compare it to the length measurements of the two remaining small block strips.

• If the small block strips' measurement is *larger* than the quilt's measurement from step 5, you will need to adjust the seams of the strip by taking them in slightly on as many blocks as needed until they are the same size.

• If the small block strip's measurement is *smaller* than the quilt's measurement, you can add narrow spacer strips of the inner border fabric to the ends of the small block strips so that the pieces will fit together.

• If these measurements are *just slightly off*, see if the shorter piece can be blocked (see Challenge 2, page 20) just a bit to make the pieces match. Be careful not to distort the strip by too much stretching.

Sew an inner border strip measuring 1½" × 6½" (or whatever your measurement in step 5 was) to each end of the two remaining small block strips. Make two. Press seam allowances toward border strips.

Make 2

·11· Recheck your measurements to ensure that the small
block strips will fit the quilt nicely. Add one of the
remaining small blocks to each end of each small
block strip.

·12· Check your measurements one more time to ensure that the inner border strips
will line up correctly. If needed, make additional small adjustments in seam allowances or by adding spacers. Sew the two small block strips to the top and bottom
of the quilt, making sure to line up the inner borders and matching centers.

Finish as desired (see pages 22-23).

Red and Black Surprise

37¼ " × 37¼ "

The Mosaic blocks were a gift from
fellow quilt guild member Alberta Kiss.

Pieced and machine-quilted by the author

❖ modern *variation*

The modern variation, STROLL IN THE COUNTRY, features blocks from an unfinished Block of the Month Club offered at my local quilt shop four or five years ago. After I had completed RED & BLACK SURPRISE and was looking for blocks for the variation quilt, I remembered this partial set. They were very busy and I wondered what would happen if I chopped them up, using the RED & BLACK SURPRISE setting. So, I took a deep breath and chopped. The large blue triangles in the center pinwheel offered a place to rest your eyes, which helped to calm down the busyness of the pieced blocks. These blocks were larger than the mosaic blocks, so I had to do some calculating to get everything to fit properly. The red, white and blue plaid inner border of STROLL IN THE COUNTRY adds a bit of zing whereas the black inner border added a frame around the pinwheel in RED & BLACK SURPRISE.

Stroll in the Country

37¼ " × 37¼ "

Pieced and machine-quilted by the author

boys are so square

I am particularly fond of this set of eight Twelve Triangles blocks. They were machine-pieced sometime in the 1920s. I wonder if these blocks were left over from a larger project (and these were the rejects), or if the maker gave up on them after making only eight blocks.

Although there is pink fabric present in these blocks, they are primarily blue and green, which made me think about a quilt for a baby boy, and the fact that the blocks were not square led to the name, BOYS ARE SO SQUARE.

✣ *shopping* list

Orphan Blocks

Eight 8" (finished size) blocks

Companion Fabrics

Center squares and side triangles: ¾ yard light background fabric
First side borders: ¼ yard light fabric
Second side borders: ½ yard medium fabric
Outside border: 1 yard dark fabric

To Finish

Batting: 47" × 59"
Backing fabric: 47" × 59"
Binding fabric: ⅜ yard

✥ *design* considerations

There is nothing square about these blocks—which amuses me, because they are a variation of the square-in-a-square quilt block! Their crookedness only makes them more delightful. I resisted the urge to tear them apart and put them back together more precisely. I accepted the way they were: crooked with cut-off corners and a few stains that would not come out completely.

Once I had pressed the blocks and squared them up to the same size, another dilemma surfaced. I only had eight blocks and I wanted to make the finished quilt baby quilt sized. I knew from previous experience that putting blocks on point adds length, so I did that, alternating the blocks with plain squares. Then I needed to add several side borders to get the desired width.

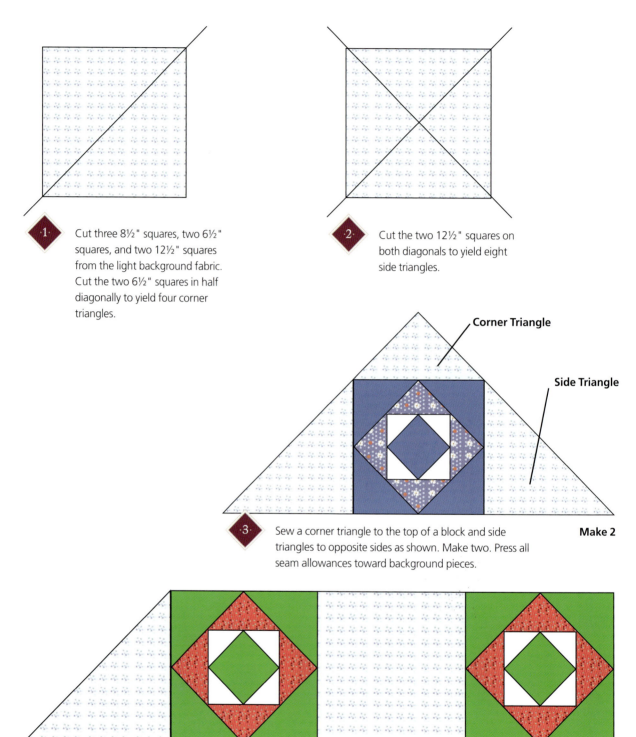

·1· Cut three 8½" squares, two 6½" squares, and two 12½" squares from the light background fabric. Cut the two 6½" squares in half diagonally to yield four corner triangles.

·2· Cut the two 12½" squares on both diagonals to yield eight side triangles.

Corner Triangle

Side Triangle

·3· Sew a corner triangle to the top of a block and side triangles to opposite sides as shown. Make two. Press all seam allowances toward background pieces.

Make 2

·4· Sew a background square between two pieced blocks. Sew a side triangle to the left side of the unit.

Make 3

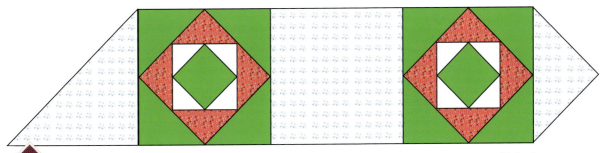

Make 2

◆5◆ On two of the units from step 4, add a corner triangle to the right side, following the diagram. Make two. Press seam allowances toward background pieces.

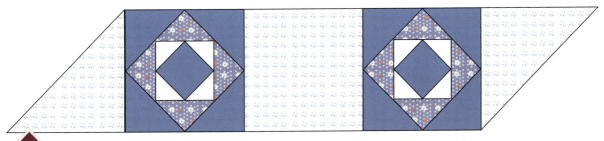

Make 1

◆6◆ On the third unit from step 4, add a side triangle to the right side of unit. Make one. Press seam allowances toward background pieces.

◆7◆ Assemble quilt units following the diagram. Press seam allowances toward background pieces.

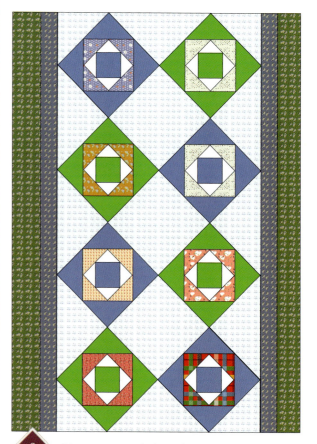

·8· Measure your quilt through the center vertically, and cut two 2½" strips of the first side border fabric by this length (ideally 45½"), piecing as needed. Sew strips to sides of the quilt, matching centers. Press seam allowances toward borders.

·9· Measure your quilt through the center vertically, and cut two 3½" strips of the second side border fabric by this length (ideally 45½"), piecing as needed. Sew strips to sides of the quilt, matching centers. Press seam allowances toward outer borders.

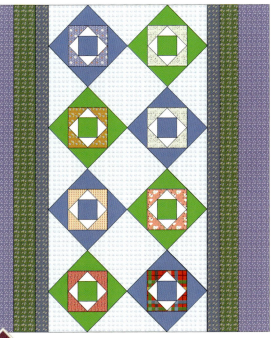

 10 Measure your quilt through the center vertically, and cut two 4½" strips of the outer border fabric by this length (ideally 45½"). Sew borders to sides of the quilt, matching centers. Press seam allowances toward outer borders.

11 Measure your quilt through the center horizontally, and cut two 4½" strips of the outer border fabric by this length (ideally 41½"), piecing as needed. Sew strips to top and bottom of quilt, matching centers.

Finish as desired (see pages 22-23).

Boys Are So Square

41" × 53"

The Twelve Triangles blocks were purchased from a garage sale (part of the author's Louetta Hoffman collection).

Pieced and machine-quilted by the author

❖ modern *variation*

In Boys Are So Square, the blocks were the central focus of the quilt, but when I began to play with a set of red and green Shoofly blocks, I experimented with color placement in the plain blocks down the center of the quilt. I found that I really liked the strong red squares down the center and balanced them with equally strong borders, including an inner blue side border; whereas in Boys Are So Square, the borders blend with the inner part of the quilt. It never fails to amaze me how fabric choice and color placement can make such a difference, even when you are working with the same basic design.

Jingle Jangle

40" × 51"

Pieced and machine-quilted by the author

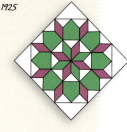

Quilt block circa 1925

lavender green

This is a wonderful set of circa 1925 Star of Bethlehem blocks. They were part of my Louetta Hoffman collection, but I don't think Louetta made them. By the 1920s, she was an accomplished quilter, but these quirky blocks are probably some of the most poorly pieced I've ever worked with! There were actually eight blocks, seven with matching fabrics and one using a different combination of fabrics. I speculate that these were the only blocks completed by the sewer who figured out that the design was too advanced for her skills, or these blocks were not good enough to be included in the actual quilt. No two blocks were the same size, nor were any of them square.

❖ *shopping* list

Orphan Blocks

Six 15" (finished size) blocks

To Finish

Batting: 60" × 80"
Backing: 60" × 80"
Binding: ⅝ yard

Companion Fabrics

2¼ yards of fabric A for side and corner triangles, framing strips for center squares of companion blocks

2 yards of fabric B for center squares of companion blocks and border

Another person might have picked out all of the seams and re-pieced the blocks or even tossed them out, but not me. I pressed them into submission, stitched up the holes, squared each mis-shapen block, and then added a border to make them all the same size. I think you'll agree that the completed quilt is very sweet, even if it isn't perfect.

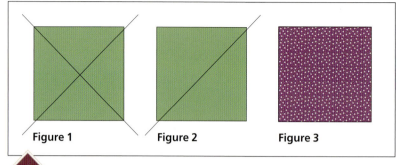

Figure 1 **Figure 2** **Figure 3**

Make 2

 Cut two 22½" squares out of fabric A. Cut squares on both diagonals to make eight side triangles (you will need only six). (Figure 1)

Cut two 11½" squares out of fabric A. Cut squares diagonally from one corner to the other to make 4 corner triangles. (Figure 2)

Cut two 10½" squares out of fabric B. These are the centers of the framed companion blocks. (Figure 3)

 Cut two 3" strips by width of fabric from fabric A. Subcut the two strips into four 3" × 10½" segments and four 3" × 15½" strips. These strips will frame the 10½" block centers from step 1.

Sew 3" × 10½" rectangles to each side of the fabric B square. Press.

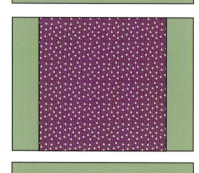

Make 2

 Sew 3" × 15½" rectangles to top and bottom. Press.

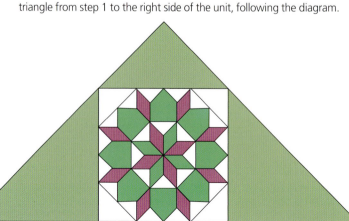

Make 2

 Sew a framed companion block between two orphan blocks. Then sew a corner triangle from step 1, figure 1 to the left side of the unit and a side triangle from step 1 to the right side of the unit, following the diagram.

Make 2

Sew two side triangles from step 1, figure 2 to the sides of an orphan block. Then sew a corner triangle from step 1 to the top of the unit, following the diagram.

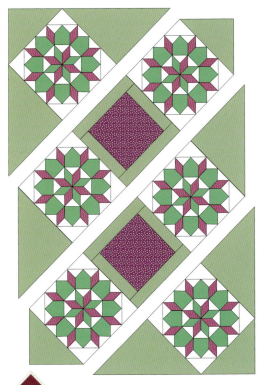

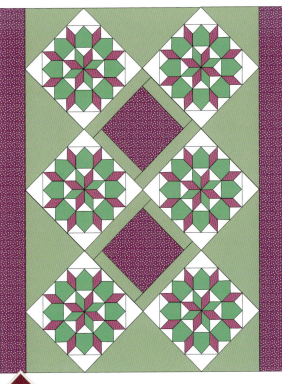

◆6◆ Sew all four sections together, following diagram.

◆7◆ Measure your quilt vertically through the center. Cut two borders 6½" by this length (ideally 63¾"), piecing as needed. Sew borders to sides of quilt, matching centers.

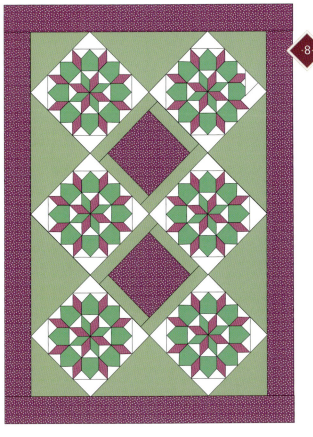

◆8◆ Measure your quilt horizontally through the center. Cut two borders 6½" by this length (ideally 54½"), piecing as needed. Sew borders to top and bottom of quilt, matching centers.

Finish as desired (see pages 22-23).

Lavender Green

54" × 75"

The Star of Bethlehem blocks were purchased from a garage sale (part of the author's Louetta Hoffman collection).

Pieced and machine-quilted by the author

❖ modern *variation*

When I created the modern variation, Caribbean Cappuccino, I made a few small changes to the Lavender Green setting. These small changes along with the fabric choices really altered the whole feeling of the quilt. I made the frames larger in the two central squares because the tan fabric calmed down the busy blue print. I also added light blue to the four corners instead of using the same background fabric throughout because it made me think of waves on the beach. Even with the busy fabrics, the blues and tans really give this quilt a calm feel.

Caribbean Cappuccino

55" × 78"

Pieced and machine-quilted by the author

Quilt block circa 1930

art deco runner

This classic 1930s appliquéd Pansy block was once again part of my Louetta Hoffman collection. Sadly, it was the only one in the collection, which made it a true orphan quilt block. I liked the simplicity of the design and the way the bloom was placed diagonally on the background square. The stylized shape of the Pansy is reminiscent of Art Deco elements, which include scallops and curves as well as stepped forms.

❖ *shopping* list

Orphan Blocks

One 9" (finished size) block

Companion Fabrics

Background: ½ yard
Framing block: ⅓ yard fabric

To Finish

Batting: 21" × 44"
Backing fabric: ¾ yard
Binding fabric: ⅜ yard

✤ *design* considerations

I like to keep a notebook and pencil beside my bed because some of my best design ideas (like this one) come to me while I am sleeping. I actually came up with this design long before I had the right quilt block to place in the center of the frame. The medallion center of the runner made me think of decorative pieces from the Art Deco period; thus, the runner was named. Once I found the orange and green appliquéd Pansy block from circa 1930, though, the design was finally complete.

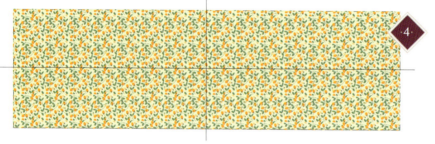

·1· Cut two 3¼" strips by the width of fabric from framing fabric. Subcut strips into two 9½" segments and two 15" segments. Sew 9½" framing segments to sides of orphan quilt block. Press seam allowances toward the frame.

·2· Sew 15" framing segments to top and bottom of orphan quilt block. Fold raw edges under 1" all the way around the block and press.

·3· Fold framed block in half on both diagonals to find the center. Press block to crease fold lines.

·4· Cut a 15½" by 38½" rectangle from main fabric. Fold main fabric rectangle in half lengthwise and widthwise to find center. Press fabric to crease fold lines.

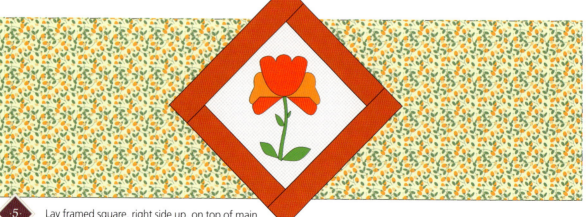

·5· Lay framed square, right side up, on top of main fabric rectangle, also right side up. Align folds to center block correctly on rectangle (the top and bottom points will stick out beyond the main fabric rectangle).

 6. Pin the framed block in place. Using your preferred method of appliqué, appliquéd the sides of framed block to main fabric rectangle (sample was machine appliquéd using clear thread and a blind hemstitch). Baste the top and bottom edges of block. When the top is complete, layer the pieces together—backing (wrong side up), batting and then the top (right side up). Baste together, paying particular attention to the top and bottom edges of the block that extend. Quilt as desired, square up the edges, and then bind.

Art Deco Runner

15" × 38"

Pansy appliquéd block part of the author's Louetta Hoffman collection

Pieced and quilted by the author

❖ modern *variation*

ART DECO RUNNER's modern variation, CELTIC ELEGANCE, has a center medallion that is square instead of set on point. I wondered what a Celtic knot would look like in the center of the same design, so I asked my friend, Mary Lee Minnis, if she could create a Celtic block for me. I never thought to ask her to put the block on point. Sometimes, design changes happen from necessity, not because of artistic choice. The elegant gold-etched fabrics really add an air of luxury to CELTIC ELEGANCE while the crisp green and orange combination in ART DECO is youthful and informal.

Celtic Elegance

15" × 38"

Block and piecing by Mary Lee Minnis

Machine-quilted by the author

ausie's girls

The four signature blocks in this quilt were created in 1936 by Ausie Shutt and her girls (see page 97). Not only do each of the blocks feature the maker's name, but also the type of block. Ausie Shutt created the Double-X. Her daughters, Mary Shutt McAlevy and Minnie Shutt, created the Evening Star and Shoo Fly blocks respectively, and her daughter-in-law, Grace Keller, created the New Album block.

❖ *shopping* list

Orphan Blocks

One 12" (finished size) block for the center

To Finish

Batting: 48" × 48"
Backing fabric: 48" × 48"
Binding fabric: ½ yard

Companion Fabrics

Corners: Four 12" (finished size) companion blocks

Center star triangles, inner border and cornerstones: 1¼ yard

Star points and outer border: 1¼ yard

Star background: 1 fat quarter fabric

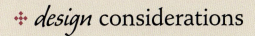

❖ *design* considerations

I treasured the four signature blocks for perhaps ten years before having enough courage and a quilt design to make them shine. I added a Dresden Plate block in the center to complement the four signature blocks. Together, these five blocks make a sweet wall quilt or child's quilt with the surprise addition of the eight-pointed star made from modern reproduction fabrics.

  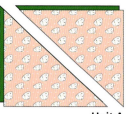 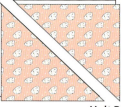

Unit A   **Unit B**

·1· Cut one 13¼" squares from the center star triangle fabric, one 13¼" square from the background fat quarter, and two 13¼" squares from the star point fabric. Draw a line diagonally from one corner to the other on the wrong side of each square.

Layer a star point fabric square and the background fabric square right sides together. Sew ¼" away from both sides of the drawn line. Repeat with the other star point fabric and the star center triangle fabric.

·2· Cut squares apart on drawn line to yield two blocks each of star point fabric/star center fabric (unit A) and star point fabric/background fabric (unit B). Press triangle seams towards star point fabric on all four sets.

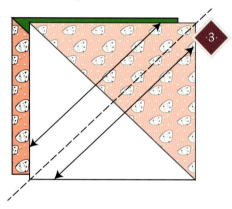

·3· Draw a diagonal line from corner to corner, crossing the seam as shown, on the wrong side of all units. Layer a unit A with a unit B, right sides together, matching the diagonal seam, so that the star point fabrics are *not* on top of each other. Sew ¼" from both sides of the drawn line.

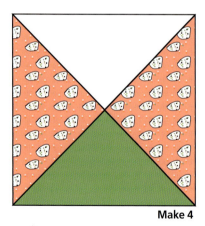

Make 4

·4· Cut squares apart along the drawn line to yield four hourglass blocks. Press seams open to reduce bulk. Square up to 12½" × 12½", if needed.

·5· Lay out the orphans with the hourglass blocks as shown. Sew the blocks together into rows and then sew the rows together to make the quilt center.

Make 4

Make 4

·6· Measure your quilt through the center both vertically and horizontally. Measurements should be the same (ideally 36½"). If your measurements are different, you may need to adjust the quilt center by slightly increasing or decreasing seam allowances between blocks. Cut four 2½" wide inner border strips and four 2½" wide outer border strips by this length (ideally 36½"). Sew each inner border strip to an outer border strip. Press.

·7· Cut twelve 2½" × 2½" outer border fabric squares and four 2½" × 2½" inner border squares (cornerstones). Sew together to make 4 four-patch units, following the diagram. Press.

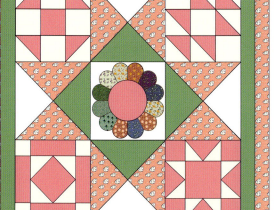

Make 2

·8· Sew the side inner/outer border strips to the sides of the quilt center, matching centers.

·9· Sew the four patch units from step 9 to the ends of the top/bottom inner/outer border strips, following diagram. Press.

·10· Sew the top and bottom inner/outer border strips to top and bottom of quilt center, matching centers. Press. Finish as desired (see pages 22-23).

Ausie's Girls

44" × 44"

The four signature blocks were purchased from an auction. The center Dresden Plate block was part of a collection of blocks given to the author by friend and fellow guild member Marsha Waite.

Pieced and quilted by the author

❖ quiltmaker
Ausie Shutt

Ausie Mary Johnston was born 21 March 1874 in Centre County, Pennsylvania. She married Walker Shutt in 1899. Ausie's husband died in a tragic work accident in 1917, leaving her with young children to raise. As a memorial to her husband, Ausie used scraps of his clothing to make a quilt.

Most likely, she taught her daughters, Minnie and Mary, to quilt. Sometime in 1936, Ausie, her two daughters and her daughter-in-law, Grace Keller, worked on a quilt project. No one knows if the four signature blocks in AUSIE'S GIRLS were left over from a larger project or if they were the beginning of a project never completed.

Signature blocks themselves began as a new trend in the 1840s because of the development of indelible ink.

Signature quilts are generally divided into two subcategories: friendship quilts and album quilts. Friendship quilts were most often scrappy, comprised of pieced quilt blocks while the album quilt was more formal, most frequently made with appliquéed quilt blocks. Appliquéd album quilts rose to popularity in the 1850s, particularly in areas around Baltimore, Maryland.

The popularity of signature quilts waned in the 1870s and was replaced with another new fad—crazy quilts. However, signature quilts did not die—there were several resurgences in the decades since the 1870s. Later signature quilts also commemorated special events or raised money for special causes.

It's possible that the four women were involved with the Ladies' Civic Club, which sponsored projects to improve the town of Boalsburg, Pennsylvania. In 1934, the Club hosted a quilt exhibit. Perhaps Ausie, Minnie, Mary and

Ausie Shutt (center) with daughters Mary (left) and Minnie (right), circa 1936. Photo courtesy of Barbara Shutt Beckwith.

Grace were involved in its planning, and these signature blocks were inspired by that event.

Ausie died 21 January 1951, at the age of 77.

If you are fortunate enough to possess a set of signature blocks, a large part of the fun is researching the blocks. With a name or several names, you can do some basic research on the Internet, using websites devoted to genealogical research and information. Census records are also a great place to start because you might find location connections among the names. If you are able to determine a location from either the blocks themselves or by researching names, you could contact the nearest historical or genealogical society to request more information on the name or names found on the blocks. Who knows? You might find a living relative with more information, photographs, or even more quilts!

happy quilt

C ross and Crown, a name straight out of Scripture, is just one of many names for this set of circa 1940 blocks. Quiltmakers used their own unique experiences to name quilt blocks, even if the block was called by a different name somewhere else.

I instantly fell in love when I saw these blocks at a Lancaster, Pennsylvania quilt show in 2007. They made me happy, so I purchased them and called them my "Happy Blocks." A year later, I turned those "Happy Blocks" into this cozy HAPPY QUILT, which is backed with fleece for cuddling.

✦ *shopping* list

Orphan Blocks

Seven 12" (finished size) blocks

Companion Fabrics

Background: Five squares of assorted light background fabrics, 19" × 19"
Inner border: ⅞ yard
Outer border: 1⅝ yard

To Finish

Batting: 57" × 74"
Backing: 57" × 74"
Binding: ⅝ yard

❖ *design* considerations

Sometimes orphan blocks have a will of their own. With HAPPY QUILT, I experienced some difficulty arranging the colors in a pleasing way. The main problem was that the green and purple fabrics kept jumping out, and I wanted the quilt to read blue and yellow. After playing with the blocks until they were satisfactorily arranged, I auditioned border fabrics, settling on the inner blue border and the pink, blue and yellow outer border with a pink plaid binding. This wasn't quite the blue and yellow color scheme that I wanted, but the blocks and I reached a happy compromise.

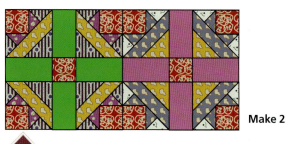

·1· Cut five 18¼" squares from the five background fabrics. Cut each square on both diagonals to make 20 triangles. Two triangles from each fabric can be set aside for another project.

Make 2

·2· Sew two orphan quilt blocks together. Make two sets. Press.

Make 2

·3· Sew a background triangle to each side of the orphan quilt block sets from step 3. Press seam allowances toward triangles.

Make 1

·4· Sew three orphan quilt blocks together with a background triangle at each end. Press seam allowances toward triangle.

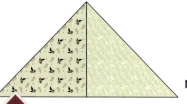

Make 2

·5· Sew two triangles together along the short edges as shown. Make two. Press.

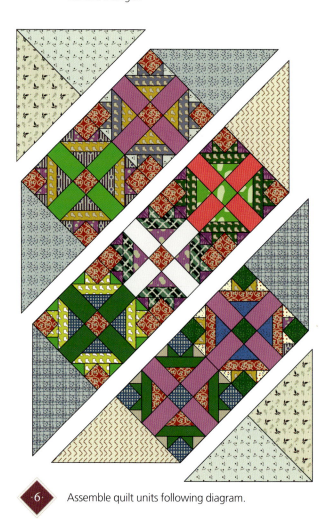

·6· Assemble quilt units following diagram.

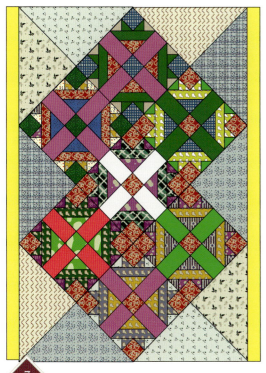

◆·7· Measure quilt through the center vertically (ideally 51½"). Cut four 3" wide strips by this length, piecing as needed. Sew borders to sides of quilt, matching centers.

◆·8· Measure quilt through the center horizontally (ideally 39½"), and cut two 3" wide strips by this length. Sew strips to the top and bottom of the quilt. Press.

Make 2

◆·9· Cut two 6½" wide strips to match the horizontal measurement from step 8 (ideally 39½"). Then cut four 3" by 6½" segments from the inner border fabric. Sew an inner border segment to each end of the outer border strips.

◆·10· Sew strips to top and bottom of quilt.

11. Measure quilt through center vertically once again (ideally 68½"), and cut four 6½" wide strips of outer border fabric by this length, piecing as needed. Sew outer border strips to sides of quilt, matching centers.

Finish as desired (see pages 22-23).

Happy Quilt

51" × 68"

The Cross and Crown blocks were purchased at a quilt show.

Pieced and quilted by the author

❖ modern *variation*

The blocks used in WATERMELON TAFFY are from an unfinished Block of the Month Sampler offered at a local quilt shop many years ago. The sampler blocks give this quilt a very different feel. The center machine-appliquéed block in WATERMELON TAFFY was a little bit smaller than the other blocks so a narrow green border was added, which actually frames the block nicely. Other differences include alternating pink and green background triangles instead of scrappy light fabrics and a more complex border treatment.

Watermelon Taffy

52" × 63"

Pieced by Cathy Laird

Machine-quilted by the author

fan fare

I really like this set of Fan blocks (when I found them amongst my Louetta Hoffman collection, they were not yet appliquéd to background squares and only a few had the pie wedges already in place). Fan shapes began making their debut in quilts during the crazy quilt fad in the late nineteenth century, possibly from an American fascination with Japanese art. The first printed fan design appeared in 1897, and the pattern was a beloved favorite by the 1930s. These blocks are from about 1950.

❖ *shopping* list

Orphan Blocks

Sixteen 7" (finished size) blocks

Companion Blocks

Nine 4" (finished size) blocks

Companion Fabrics

Sashing and border corner squares:
1 yard fabric
Border: yard fabric

To Finish

Batting fabric: 54" × 54"
Backing fabric: 54" × 54"
Binding fabric: ½ yard

❖ *design* considerations

There were only fifteen fans, but I needed sixteen blocks for this design, so I delved into my stash of vintage and antique fabrics and made one more block. I had to take apart one fan in order to make a pattern for the additional block. It was a very simple process. Bet you can't guess which one of the fan blocks that I made! The addition of the four patches makes this quilt quite eye-catching with a lot of movement.

Cut 5 rectangles from each strip, 4½" × 7½"

Cut 4 squares, 4½" × 4½"

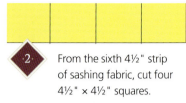

 Cut six 4½" by width of fabric strips of sashing fabric. Subcut five strips into five 4½" × 7½" rectangles for a total of 25 sashing rectangles. (You only need 24 for this quilt.)

From the sixth 4½" strip of sashing fabric, cut four 4½" × 4½" squares.

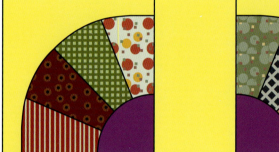

Make 8

Make 6

 Sew a sashing rectangle between two 7" (finished size) blocks. Press seam allowances toward sashing.

4· Sew a sashing cornerstone between two sashing rectangles. Make six (set two aside until step 6). Set aside the rest of the sashing rectangles until step 7.

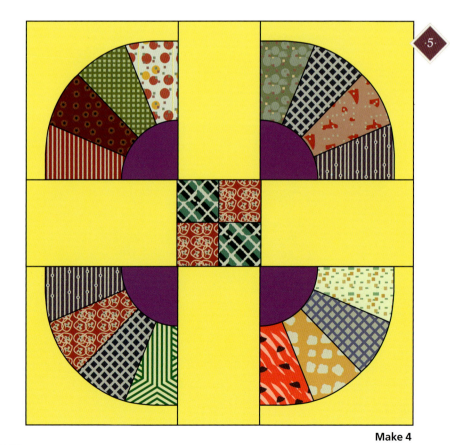

5· Assemble Fan square sections by sewing one segment from step 4 between two segments from step 3. Press. Make four.

Make 4

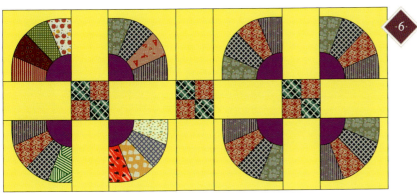

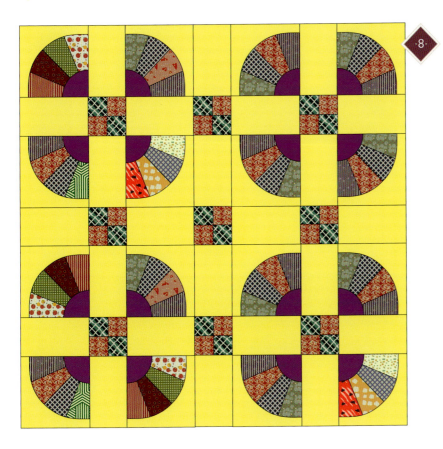

•6•
Sew a sashing and cornerstone section (the ones set aside in step 4) between two Fan squares.

Make 2

•7•
Assemble center horizontal sashing section by alternating four 4½" × 7½" sashing strips (set aside from step 4) with three companion blocks.

Make 1

•8•
Sew horizontal sashing section (from step 7) between the two fan square sections. Press seam allowances toward sashing.

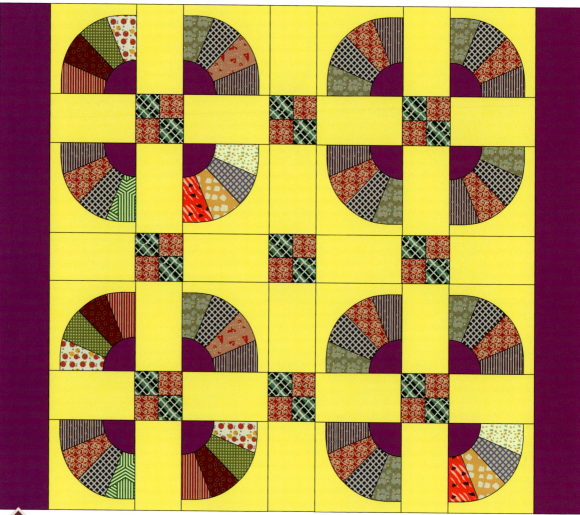

 ·9· Measure your quilt horizontally and vertically through the center (ideally 40½"). Cut four 4½" strips of border fabric to this measurement. Sew border strips to sides of quilt, matching center of border to center of quilt. Press seam allowances toward borders.

·10· Sew four 4½" × 4½" border corner squares (from step 2) to the ends of the top and bottom border strips. Press seam allowance toward borders.

Make 2

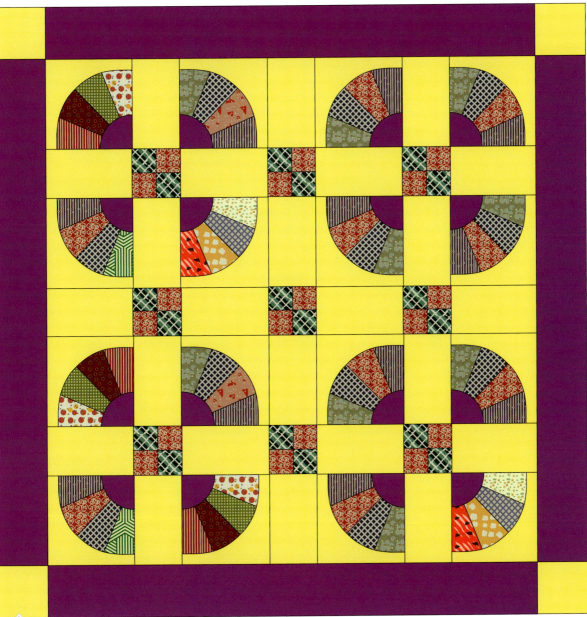

 Sew top and bottom borders to quilt, matching border center to quilt center. Finish as desired (see pages 22-23).

Fan Fare

48" × 48"

The Fan blocks and Four Patch blocks were purchased from a garage sale (part of the author's Louetta Hoffman collection)

Pieced and machine-quilted by the author

❖ modern *variation*

Most likely at first glance (or even second), you didn't realize that Screamin' Mimi was the same basic design as Fan Fare. Look closely. Screamin' Mimi deftly uses angles and wild fabrics to shout "Look at me!" while Fan Fare uses gentle curves, a solid yellow background and a soft floral border to whisper "Hello." Fan Fare is visually divided into four quadrants, while Screamin' Mimi uses darker sashing strips and unpieced cornerstones to provide a little order to the topsy-turvy pieced bouquet blocks. A narrow inner border keeps the disorganization from spilling into the border, which is wider in order to showcase the wonderful floral ribbon fabric. All in all, Screamin' Mimi is aptly named.

Screamin' Mimi

41" × 41"

Pieced by Mary Lee Minnis

Machine-quilted by the author

Quilt block circa 1955

my friend sue

When I went with my quilt guild to the 2007 Lancaster Pennsylvania quilt show, I wasn't expecting to find any orphan blocks. I was pleasantly surprised to find several vendors selling antique/vintage fabrics, blocks, tops and completed quilts. These sweet blocks were among my purchases.

The Sunbonnet Sue pattern is known by many names, but one thing is certain, it's one of the most recognized patterns in quilting. Though girls with bonnet-shaded faces were seen in art and embroidery designs in the late 1800s, Sunbonnet Sue's distinctive design can be attributed to Bertha Corbett Melcher, who wrote and illustrated a book called *The Sunbonnet Babies* in 1900.

❖ *shopping* list

Orphan Blocks

Eight 12" (finished size) blocks

To Finish

Batting: 70" × 94"
Backing fabric: 70" × 94"
Binding fabric: ⅔ yard

Companion Fabrics

3 yards background fabric

1½ yards fabric A (pink) for Four Patch blocks, inner border, and outer border corner squares

2 yards fabric B (blue) for Four Patch blocks, outer border, and inner border corner squares

112

❖ design considerations

There were definitely some things I had to take into consideration when working with these blocks. One of the biggest issues is that they were all made out of the same two fabrics on a muslin background—this limited companion fabric choices. I settled on a soft pink, blue and muslin color scheme. I wanted the pink and blue fabrics to complement (not overpower) the Sues, so the squares could not be too large and the fabrics could not be too busy. The effect of the alternating chains adds interest to the quilt without taking away from the Sues.

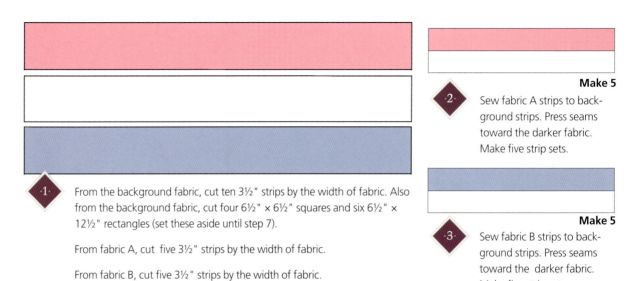

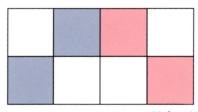

Make 5

·2· Sew fabric A strips to background strips. Press seams toward the darker fabric. Make five strip sets.

·1· From the background fabric, cut ten 3½" strips by the width of fabric. Also from the background fabric, cut four 6½" × 6½" squares and six 6½" × 12½" rectangles (set these aside until step 7).

From fabric A, cut five 3½" strips by the width of fabric.

From fabric B, cut five 3½" strips by the width of fabric.

Make 5

·3· Sew fabric B strips to background strips. Press seams toward the darker fabric. Make five strip sets.

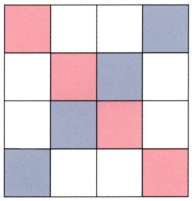

·4· Cut 48 3½" segments from both the fabric A strip sets and the fabric B strip sets.

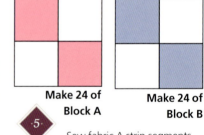

Make 24 of Block A   **Make 24 of Block B**

·5· Sew fabric A strip segments together to yield 24 Block A blocks. Sew fabric B strip segments together to yield 24 Block B blocks.

Make 10

·6· From the A and B blocks, make the following: Make 7 Double Four Patch blocks (as shown). Make 10 half-Double Four Patch blocks (as shown).

Make 7

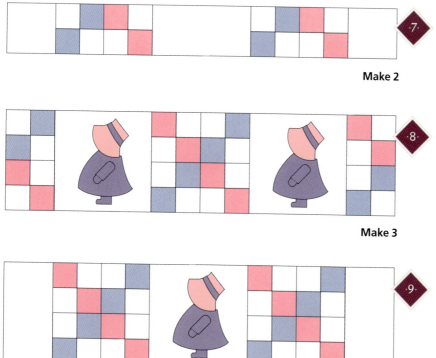

Make 2

·7·

Sew a background rectangle from step 1 between two half-Double Four Patch blocks. Then sew a background square to each end of this unit. Make two. Press seam allowances toward rectangles.

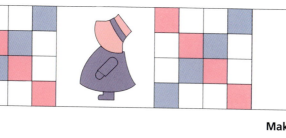

Make 3

·8·

Sew a Double Four Patch block between two orphan quilt blocks. Then sew a half Double Four Patch block to each end of this unit. Make three strip sets. Press seam allowances toward orphan blocks.

Make 2

·9·

Sew an orphan block between two Double Four Patch blocks. Then sew a background rectangle to each end of the unit. Make two strip sets. Press seam allowances toward orphan blocks and end rectangles.

·10·

Sew rows together, following diagram. Press.

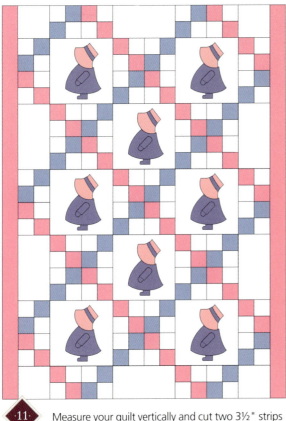

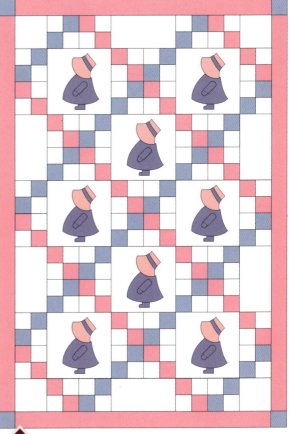

◆11◆ Measure your quilt vertically and cut two 3½" strips of fabric A by this measurement (ideally 72½"), piecing as needed. Sew strips to sides of the quilt, matching centers. Press seam allowances toward borders.

◆12◆ Measure your quilt center horizontally and cut two 3½" strips of fabric A by this measurement (ideally 48½"), piecing as needed. From fabric B, cut four 3½" squares for cornerstones. Press seam allowances toward border. Sew squares to ends of border strips. Sew strips to top and bottom of quilt, matching centers, and press.

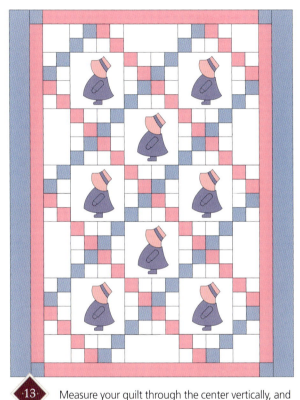

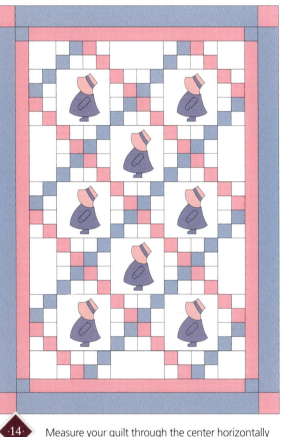

·13· Measure your quilt through the center vertically, and cut two 5½" strips of fabric B to this measurement (ideally 78½"). Sew strips to sides of the quilt, matching centers. Press seam allowances toward borders.

·14· Measure your quilt through the center horizontally and cut two 5½" strips from fabric B by this measurement (ideally 54½"). From fabric A, cut four 5½" squares for cornerstones. Sew squares to ends of border strips. Press seam allowances toward borders. Sew strips to top and bottom of quilt, matching centers.

Finish as desired (see pages 22-23).

My Friend Sue

64" × 88"

The Sunbonnet Sue blocks were purchased from a
vendor at a quilt show in Lancaster, PA in 2007.

Pieced by the author

Machine-quilted by Barb Shuck and Cindy Beggs

❖ modern *variation*

Cowboys Under the Stars has a few subtle differences that really change the look of the quilt. The background of the Double Nine Patch blocks is a light fabric while star backgrounds and side/top/bottom background rectangles are red. The inner blue border is narrower and repeats in the outer border corner squares. While My Friend Sue is sweet and soft, Cowboys Under the Stars is rough and ready. Two distinct quilts, one basic design.

Cowboys Under the Stars

62 " × 62 "

Pieced by the author

Machine-quilted by Cathy Laird

119

Evening Star
Mrs Wm McAlevy
1936

the orphanage

W hen one thinks about the term orphanage, it's not uncommon to picture children with stories—orphanages aren't generally thought of as positive places, but that is all about to change. Turn the page to check out The Orphanage, a gallery of completed orphan block quilts and other orphan block projects.

Now that you know how to find your own orphan blocks, clean and repair them, and select appropriate settings, let the fun begin!

Gather up your orphans, decide on a setting, and take them to your local quilt shop. Pick out the perfect companion fabrics. Hurry home and start sewing. Once you begin rescuing orphan quilt blocks, soon you'll have your very own orphanage populated with happy orphan quilts. What are you waiting for?

Honoring Louetta

By Cathey Laird

These three Old Maid's Puzzle blocks were hand-pieced by Louetta Shoemaker Hoffman sometime during the 1930s. I challenged Cathey to "create something" with them. In order to honor Louetta's traditional hand-piecing, Cathey hand-quilted the project. She selected a solid navy fabric to frame the blocks while a coordinating reproduction fabric and muslin created the half-square triangles. The outside border was also a reproduction fabric, and a solid red binding completed the charming runner.

Flowerbox

By the author

I had several stacks of wonderful Grandmother's Flower Garden blocks from the 1930s and 1940s, but I didn't think I could ever imagine myself hand sewing these flowers together with little green hexagons in between them. So, the next best thing was to turn the raw edges under and machine-appliqué them to a background fabric. I chose a creamy yellow background and a green and yellow floral for the border because they complimented the yellow and green in the flower blocks.

Elegant Evening Bag

By the author

How often can you take one—just one—quilt block and make a great project with it? The Dresden Plate block was part of a collection of blocks given to me by my friend and fellow guild member Marsha Waite. This bag is versatile, easy to construct, and makes a wonderful gift for a special quilting friend or for yourself.

Lucy and Her Doll Quilts

By Leslie Lattner

Lucy, her doll quilt, and her tiny quilt began as four circa 1910 Half Square Triangle blocks. Leslie carefully took the blocks apart and reset the half square triangles into economy blocks. These blocks became the larger doll quilt. While working on the doll quilt, Leslie thought that if she had been making this quilt a hundred years ago, it would have been made for a doll. So she decided to make a doll, and when she was making the doll, she wondered why couldn't she let her doll make her own "quilt" too? As a finishing touch, Lucy's hair was cut from the fringe on Leslie's vintage rag rug in her dining room.

Market Day Expandable Bag

By Cheryl Weiderspahn

This nifty bag uses orphan Four Patch blocks from circa 1900 to the 1930's with a reproduction indigo fabric. It is slip-covered in vinyl to protect the quilt blocks—this allows appreciation and the bag to actually be used. The size of the bag is adjustable, using a loop and button system. The handle is also adjustable. Vintage buttons close the top and add interest to the bag.

Floral Lattice Table Runner

By Mary Lee Minnis

These circa 1980s floral appliqué blocks were purchased at a neighbor's yard sale. Because the neighbor was also a quilter, Mary Lee asked if she had made the blocks, but the neighbor said that she had found in a box she had bought at an auction. One block was missing the center appliqué and was smaller than the other blocks. Mary Lee appliquéd a center circle and cleverly added a narrow border to the smaller center block to make it the correct size. The perfect finishing touch was a lattice-style border, which made a nice setting for the flowers. The border was inspired from a quilt in a magazine Mary Lee had once seen.

❖ index

❖ Every quilt has a story to tell

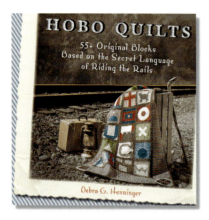

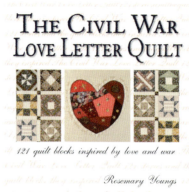

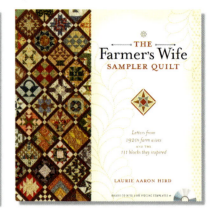

Hobo Quilts

55+ Original Blocks Based on the Secret Language of Riding the Rails

Debra G. Henninger

Explore the fascinating world of Depression-era hobo culture through the hidden language of signs and symbols, all translated into 55 original quilt blocks and 20 gorgeous projects. Let *Hobo Quilts* take you on a journey to the times when railways were the lifeblood of America, transporting goods from city to city and carrying people in search of a better life.

paperback; 8" × 8"; 256 pages

ISBN-10: 1-4402-0412-8

ISBN-13: 978-1-4402-0412-8

SRN: Z5432

The Civil War Love Letter Quilt

121 Quilt Blocks Inspired by Love and War

Rosemary Youngs

This book is a history book, quilting guide and touching tales of the love shared by Civil War soldiers, their sweethearts and families. Using the same innovative approach as other books in the popular letter and diary quilt-book series by Rosemary Youngs, this new guide showcases 121 different paper-pieced block patterns with the actual letters.

paperback; 8" × 8"; 288 pages

ISBN-10: 0-89689-487-8

ISBN-13: 978-0-89689-487-7

SRN: Z0751

The Farmer's Wife Sampler Quilt

Letters from 1920s Farm Wives and the 111 Blocks They Inspired

Laurie Aaron Hird

In 1922, *The Farmer's Wife* magazine posed this question to their readers: "If you had a daughter of marriageable age, would you, in light of your own experience, have her marry a farmer?" The best answers to this question are included in this book, along with the traditional quilt blocks they inspired.

paperback; 8" × 8"; 256 pages; CD-rom with PDF templates

ISBN-10: 0-89689-828-8

ISBN-13: 978-0-89689-828-8

SRN: Z2991

These and other fine Krause Publications titles are available at your local craft retailer, bookstore or online supplier, or visit our website at www.mycraftivitystore.com.